D0610714

LOVE LIFE FOR EVERY MARRIED COUPLE

How to fall in love, stay in love, rekindle your love

Ed Wheat, MD

Marshall Pickering
An Imprint of HarperCollinsPublishers

Marshall Pickering is an Imprint of
HarperCollins*Religious*
Part of HarperCollins*Publishers*
77–85 Fulham Palace Road,
London W6 8JB

First published in Great Britain
in 1984 by Marshall Morgan and Scott,
subsequently Marshall Pickering

5 7 9 10 8 6 4

A catalogue record for this book is
available from the British Library

ISBN 0 551 01141 6

Printed in Great Britain by
HarperCollinsManufacturing Glasgow

Contents

Introduction

When I began my practice as a family physician in the beautiful little community of Springdale, Arkansas, more than twenty-five years ago, I had no plans of becoming either a certified sex therapist or a marriage counselor. And since I was totally unfamiliar with the Bible, the possibility of becoming a biblical counselor of course never occurred to me.

But I soon discovered that a family doctor has to treat many problems that cannot be resolved medically. Marriage counseling that improved my patients' home life evolved from my desire to meet their needs.

Then about twenty years ago God used a patient who was concerned about my eternal well-being to introduce me to His Son, the Lord Jesus Christ. From the day I became a Christian I poured my life into learning what the Word of God had to say to me as a husband and father, then putting it into practice as best I knew how. This has had unexpected and far-reaching results.

Today I have the privilege of counseling people from all over the world in the area of love, sex, and marriage from the biblical and medical viewpoints. Our published materials, counseling cassette albums, and seminars evoke a constant stream of letters and requests for personal counsel. The issue on the minds of most people is not sex, but the core problem: love, or the lack of it and their longing for it.

In a typical week these burdens are expressed:

A letter from the African continent asks if there is any way a couple can *learn* to love each other.

A husband and wife telephone, bewildered and heavy-hearted: "We are married, and as Christians we do not want to resort to divorce. But there is *no love* in our marriage. What can we do?"

"I know I should go back to my wife," a new Christian admits in counseling, "but I don't care for her. Honestly, I never have."

"I'm so torn inside, so disappointed in our marriage," a missionary writes.

A wife confides, "We are both born-again Christians. But my husband doesn't see that it is possible for love to be rekindled in our marriage. I know our God is big enough to handle that!"

The good news I share with all these people and the good news I want to share with you is that you and your marriage partner can have a thrilling love relationship, more wonderful than any romance secular literature has ever written or filmed, *if you will develop it in God's way.*

Many of the principles put forth in this book were tested and proven in a two-year period of marital stress at the beginning of my Christian life when my lovely wife Gaye and our three young daughters were unresponsive both to the gospel and to me. (I am sure they were wondering what had happened to their husband and father as they saw me change so drastically before their eyes.) I have always been grateful for that heartbreaking experience of prolonged rejection, for this drove me to the Word of God to learn exactly what I should do. I learned that it was my responsibility to *love* my wife the way Christ loved me. Many times I did not feel like loving her, for rejection, even quiet, courteous rejection, is hard to handle. But I did it out of obedience to God. I found that as I put the principles of the Bible into practice and as I learned how to really love my wife, this became pleasure as well as responsibility. Obedience took on the bright colors of joy!

Introduction

As I slowly became the husband God had designed me to be, my wife began to respond with love just as God had planned and promised. When she trusted the Lord Jesus Christ as her personal Savior, it was the real beginning of our own love affair as God had planned it from ages past. We honestly fell in love with each other and found through firsthand experience that God has a genuine *romantic* love rooted in the reality of *agape* love for the husband and wife who will take His counsel seriously.

Our love affair, born out of commitment, encompasses far more than that now. The thrill of romance, the pleasure of friendship, the tranquillity of belonging, the sweetness of intimacy—in fact, all the aspects of love discussed in this book have become an integral part of our marriage. Not because Gaye and I are in some way unique. Certainly, no one would be likely to include a middle-aged doctor and his wife among the world's great lovers. Rather, my point is that the same principles we have used in our marriage will work in yours. They work because they are grounded in biblical truth.

Our prayer is that this book will be used in your life, not just to hold your marriage together, but also to unite you and your mate as lovers in a relationship that becomes more wonderful every day.

1

A Love Affair:
It Can Happen to You!

This book is about love and marriage: *your* marriage and the love affair that *you* can experience with your own husband or wife.

Most people think of a love affair as a passionate interlude between a man and woman who are not married—at least not to each other. The world for centuries has tried to convince people of the notion that secretive adulterous love is more exciting than love in marriage. But the dictionary defines *love affair* as "an affinity between two persons . . . a particular experience of being in love." The particular experience we are concerned with is the wonderful life-long love affair God designed for husband and wife. He has provided all the pleasures known to man in their normal, healthy, satisfying form, and as the Creator of marriage and the Author of love His provision includes a love affair full of thrills and joy and lasting satisfaction for *every* couple, not just a favored few.

Of course, it is up to each of us to discover this design for our marriage through a careful searching of the Bible and a willingness to follow the principles, instructions, and examples we find there. My purpose in writing this book is to help you, both with the search and the practical application of the truths discovered, so that you can begin to experience all that God has for you in your marriage.

Shining through the scriptural principles and patterns you will find one basic, attitude-transforming truth:

It is God's will in every marriage that the couple love each other with an absorbing spiritual, emotional, and physical attraction that continues to grow throughout their lifetime together.

Another fact follows logically from this great truth: *It is possible for any Christian couple to develop this love relationship in their marriage because it is in harmony with God's express will.*

Because He is the One who made us, who conceived the idea of marriage and ordained it for our blessing, who gave us the potential for love, He is the One who knows best how to build love into marriage. He must be intimately involved in all our efforts to develop the kind of marriage that pleases Him. As we follow His principles and put His concepts into practice, we can begin to experience the marriage that He planned for us from the beginning, filled with "the blaze of newness and the sweet assurance of sameness" all our days.

As a Christian marriage counselor who accepts the Bible as the final authority, I do not offer my patients mere sympathy or set forth pet ideas that may or may not work. The principles I offer are solid biblical principles that will always work when applied properly to individual problems. I have found God's Word, the Bible, to be eternally true and totally dependable. Cultures change; lifestyles fluctuate; modes of thought come and go with the passing of time. But God's principles do not change and human behavior does not really change either. Under the sophisticated exterior of modern man and woman, the same sinful, unworkable patterns of behavior operate with destructive force just as they did in the days of Adam and Eve or Abraham and Sarah. Ancient peoples had the same tendencies to wrongdoing and the same inner desires and needs that you and I have today Because neither God nor man has essentially changed since the dawn of time, the principles of living spelled out in the Bible are completely relevant to marriage today.

Do you see what this means to you in coping with life in the last two decades of the twentieth century? You have not been left to figure out the solutions on your own or to wonder if your behavio responses are right or wrong. You do not have to indulge in wishful thinking about unsatisfactory relationships. You are told in the Bible what to do about them and you are given every resource you need in order to do those things that will lead to your blessing and happiness. You and I can be affirmative, realistic, and objective about the problems that invade our lives because we are dealing with unshakable truth.

Perhaps this seems idealistic to you in view of the life you are leading with your husband or wife. You may be thinking, "Sounds good. But Dr. Wheat doesn't know what *our* marriage is like!"

Please note that we have titled this book, "Love-Life for *every* married couple." This means you! Because hundreds of couples have discussed their marriages with me, I understand the varied and difficult situations that can arise between two people in marriage. Some are heartbreaking; some are perplexing and unbelievably complicated. But none is beyond solution.

It will be helpful for you at this point to diagnose your own situation and to determine what you would like your relationship to be. Deciding where you are and where you should be is a first step in the direction of constructive change. One or more of the following statements will probably describe your marital situation, so put a mental checkmark where it belongs.

( ) We have a good marriage now, but we want to continue to grow in love for each other.

( ) We have never been in love, not even when first married.

( ) We have lost the love that we once felt for each other.

( ) Frankly, I am no longer in love with my partner.

( ) My partner is indifferent or seems to love someone else.

( ) We do care about each other, but our marriage is dull.

( ) I would like to know what I can do to improve our relationship.

( ) I want to restore our love and save our marriage, but my partner is uncooperative.

( ) My partner wants a divorce.
( ) We have serious problems but are agreed on trying to save our marriage.
( ) Both of us want to learn how to fall in love with each other.
( ) We're newlyweds who want to build a love that will last and become more enjoyable all the time.

Let me encourage you now about the future of your marriage. The relationship you would like to have *can happen,* but not by accident. An intimate relationship seldom improves spontaneously, and a troubled relationship almost never gets better on its own. I have no easy overnight cures to offer you, no happiness pills to transform your marriage automatically. But if you read this book carefully and consistently follow the prescriptions I give you, you are going to learn how to love in such a way that there will be a responding love from your partner. If you have a good relationship now, it will become so much better that you will be thrilled and amazed.

Love can come to you at *any* age in *any* stage of your marriage if you are willing to open the door and invite it into your relationship. No matter how bad your marital situation seems to be, you and your partner can fall in love with each other all over again—or maybe for the first time. If you've been wavering on the edge of a traumatic divorce, you can rekindle your love. You can learn how to handle the most difficult problems in such a way that your marriage will become rooted in love—stabilized and strong enough to withstand the stresses of a lifetime. Even if you are trying to save your marriage all by yourself, without any cooperation from your partner, *it can happen.* When they are properly and consistently applied, there are no exceptions, no unique cases where God's eternal concepts will fail.

I hope that you will approach this book as a counseling manual, rather than just another book to be read lightly at your leisure. These chapters contain the vital, detailed information every married couple needs in order to build love, restore love, and preserve the marriage from forces that would destroy it. A manual is a handy guide or reference book to show you *what* to do and *how* to do it. It implies action. You know that desired results will come from doing, not dreaming. So act upon the practical advice you find here, remembering that it is based on specific biblical instructions as to thought, attitude, and behavior. This is precisely the same counsel that my private patients receive. I hope you will look on it as my personal message to you, just as though I were talking to you in my office. I write with the prayer that you and your partner will learn to love each other in such a way that a world starving for the reality of love can see it manifested through your marriage.

In these pages you will meet people with problems similar to your own. Their stories stand as they told them to me. In all cases I have changed their names and unimportant details in order to protect their privacy.

Allison is just one example. She had been married for thirty years, and although she was a devout Christian, she was struggling with the temptation to divorce her husband because of longstanding problems. He had ignored his financial responsibilities; he had ignored her feelings. One thing above all others troubled her: throughout their long marriage she had never lived in a completed house!

As she described it to me, "There are always building materials in every corner and against the walls. It is a frustration to try to keep house and is so humiliating to me. I no longer will invite people in when they come to the door. I feel like going and hiding. As a younger person I always had hope that some day things would get finished, but when I got to be fifty and it was still the same, I lost hope. I knew that for the rest of my life it would always be the same. At fifty-four a man does not change his whole pattern of living. When you mentioned making our bedroom a love nest, it hurt, because I've always pictured something like that. But how could I with unfinished floors, unfinished walls, and everything makeshift?"

After Allison encountered the love-life concepts that I communicate at every opportunity, she was led by the Lord to make a commitment to learn to love her husband. The process began with a choice of her will and it proceeded through the various stages of restoring love to their relationship. Each step involved another decision to do things in God's way. The result has been what Allison calls "a miracle" in their marriage. Today she says, "I really do *feel* love for my husband now, and my desire for sex is renewed. In the past sex was the last thing I had any interest in. But now that I love my husband I really want to please him in our physical union too."

Allison can be assured that as she continues to love her husband according to biblical principles and patterns, significant changes will occur in him also. Her love already is providing a tremendous motivation for change. At fifty-four—or any other age—a man *can* change his pattern of living with the resources of God at his disposal. This story is not finished yet, but the "miracle" of love has already appeared to bless their marriage.

Allison says, "I know so many miserable, unhappy women who are still fighting their situation. My heart goes out to them. Please encourage them. . . ."

My encouragement is this: I see these miracles happening in marriages all the time. You and your partner can have a wonderful love affair. You can cause it to happen.

2

Discoveries:
The False and the True

As a mathematics major in college I learned that if you do not start with the right premise in problem solving, there is no way you can come up with the right answer. So when I became a Christian, I studied the Bible like a mathematician. That is, I spent more time in the first three chapters of Genesis than any other part of Scripture because I knew that these chapters formed the foundation for everything else in the Bible. I discovered that here in capsule form was the essence of God's truth concerning man and woman and their relationship with God and with each other; here I could begin to understand myself and my wife and to find God's perfect design for our marriage and His purpose for our life together.

So like a mathematician, I plunged into the painstaking study of these seed chapters, knowing that I had to build my life and marriage on the right premises in order to come out right at the end. The outcome has been more wonderful than I expected—a beautiful marriage, a godly home, and a life ministry with the opportunity to show many other couples how to find happiness together by following God's original plan.

Of course, in order to establish an approach to marriage based on Genesis truth, I had to unlearn some concepts I had developed earlier in life. But I could do this because I knew I had accurate information; I could replace wrong ideas with the right ones and then live by them in confidence. I found that I could depend on this truth, that it would never lead me into making bad decisions or giving bad counsel.

How about you? What has shaped your thinking about marriage? Can you depend on it?

I want you to carefully consider the underlying assumptions that govern your attitudes toward marriage and love. Some may be false; some may be true. It is essential for you to determine which premises are correct, which are worth building on, and which concepts should be discarded because they are false and therefore unworkable, even potentially harmful.

A couple I will call Dean and Carol had to come to this place after many years as active Christians in a large evangelical church. Carol regarded her husband as "a wonderful, gentle man" and a good father to their teen-age sons. Their life together was "comfortable." If the thrill seemed to be gone from their relationship, Carol attributed that to twenty years of marriage and their age—a bit past forty.

Then her world was shaken on its foundations when Dean admitted his involvement in an affair with a young woman who worked with him in the church's music ministry. Dean said the affair had ended, but a close Christian friend counseled Carol to divorce him without delay because, as she warned, "Adultery kills a marriage. And it's not right to let yourself be used as a door mat."

While Carol, feeling bewildered and betrayed, withdrew from Dean, the young woman kept on actively pursuing him. Dean had met with the deacons to confess his wrongdoing, but now he became reluctant to attend church with his wife and sons. The church leaders regarded this as proof of Dean's insincerity, and they predicted to Carol that the marriage could not be saved because "Dean is just not right with God."

Dean, deeply depressed, began considering a job transfer to another part of the country for a period of ten months or more. He explained to Carol, "The separation will help us to know if we really love each other, or not." Carol's confidante reacted with angry advice, saying, "Just pack his bags and leave them

22

on the front steps. The sooner he goes, the better!''

When Carol told me her story, I was impressed by the fact that all the people involved in this painful situation claimed to be believers in Jesus Christ who recognized His Word as truth: the wife, the husband, the other woman, the counseling friend, and the church leaders. Yet each of these, in his or her own way, had displayed a lack of knowledge of the biblical principles that could preserve and heal this marriage. So many important biblical principles concerning marriage, love, forgiveness, and restoration were violated or ignored that it is no wonder that Dean and Carol both felt "frozen" into the tragic event and were unable to move on beyond it.

Unfortunately, this is a typical story. I have heard it many times with minor variations on the basic theme. I share it with you because so much can be learned from it.

As I worked with Carol, she began taking a long look at her own thinking and behavior patterns. How valid were her actions and reactions during the crisis and what had prompted them? Were her decisions being shaped by faulty human advice or by the eternal counsels of God? What basic assumptions were guiding her thinking? Were these premises true or false?

Then something very interesting happened to Carol. When she turned to the Word of God, determined to follow His counsel wherever it led, and to leave the results with Him, the unbiblical advice she had received faded out of her thinking, and she began to see clearly the false and the true. She found that there was total disagreement between the Bible and the world's system of thinking on marriage and divorce, and that she had almost been tricked by Satan, the master hypocrite, into believing his lies concerning her marriage. She discovered that Satan can work through even the most well-meaning Christian who takes the human viewpoint on marriage instead of God's clear scriptural teaching. She also learned that when men and women react according to their natural inclinations, they will usually make the wrong decision.

As she described it, both she and Dean had fallen into a pit of muddled thinking, mixed-up feelings, and wrong reactions. Only the truth could set them free. Together they began the relearning process, and they started with Genesis 1-3.

Every married couple needs to know the real truth concerning marriage, but it will never be found in the teachings or examples of the present world system. The best this world can offer is a low-cost, no-fault divorce obtained through the local department store—a new convenience for thousands of people blundering in and out of marriage as though it were a revolving door. It took the words of one social critic to put the situation into clear, hard perspective. He said, "In the 1970s, divorce became the *natural outcome* of marriage!"

If divorce is now accepted, even expected, as the natural result of marriage, this is a chilling heritage for the 80s and 90s. But we certainly do not have to adopt it in our thinking. Bible-believing Christians in every culture, in every age, have found the wisdom and strength to move upstream against the current of prevailing life styles. Note that the scriptural wisdom comes first: then the strength to go against popular opinion, no matter how powerful.

Let me take you on the scriptural tour that Dean and Carol took in their search for foundational truth on which to build their marriage. We'll begin at the beginning with the creation of male and female. Our purpose: to understand marriage as God ordained it in contrast to the opinions of the world around us. We need to look at these verses in Genesis as though we have never seen them before; we will look at them not as cliches but as truth for our individual lives.

1) The idea of male and female was God's idea.

"So God created man in his own image, in the image of God created he him; male and female created he them" (Genesis 1:27).

Genesis 1 declares the fact of man's creation while Genesis 2 reveals the process by which this occurred. Here in the first chapter we find the fundamental truth that is so essential to the appreciation of marriage—that God made male and female for His own good purposes. It seems too obvious to mention, but perhaps it should be pointed out that the creation of two kinds of people—men and women—was not a dark conspiracy to thwart the ambitions of the women's liberation movement. It was scarcely a put-down for women. Indeed, it became a testimonial, for creation was incomplete without woman. In a loving, amazing, creative act, the almighty God conceived the wonderful mysteries of male and female, masculinity and femininity, to bring joy into our lives. Think how colorless, how one-dimensional a world would be in which there was only your sex! Who would want to live in an all-male world or an all-female world? Or, for that matter, in a unisex world where all signs of gender were ignored or suppressed? The person who refuses to see and rejoice in the fundamental differences between male and female will never taste the divine goodness God planned for marriage.

2) Marriage was designed by God to meet the first problem of the human race: loneliness.

And the LORD God said, It is not good that the man should be alone; I will make him an help meet for him. And out of the ground the LORD God formed every beast of the field, and every fowl of the air; and brought them unto Adam to see what he would call them: and whatsoever Adam called every living creature, that was the name thereof. And Adam gave names to all cattle, and to the fowl of the air, and to every beast of the field; but for Adam there was not found an help meet for him. And the LORD God caused a deep sleep to fall upon Adam, and he slept: and he took one of his ribs, and closed up the flesh instead thereof; and the rib, which the LORD God had taken from man, made he a woman, and brought her unto the man (Genesis 2:18-22).

Picture this one man in a perfect environment, but alone. He had the fellowship of God and the company of birds and animals. He had an interesting job, for he was given the task of observing, categorizing, and naming all living creatures. But he was alone. God observed that this was "not good." So a wise and loving Creator provided a perfect solution. He made another creature, like the man and yet wondrously unlike him. She was taken from him, but she complemented him. She was totally suitable for him—spiritually, intellectually, emotionally, and physically. According to God, she was designed to be his "helper." This term *helper* refers to a beneficial relationship where one person aids or supports another person as a friend and ally. Perhaps you have thought of a helper as a subordinate, a kind of glorified servant. You will see the woman's calling in a new light when you realize that the same Hebrew word for *help* is used of God Himself in Psalm 46:1 where He is called our *helper*, "a very present help in trouble."

Marriage always begins with a need that has been there from the dawn of time, a need for companionship and completion that God understands. Marriage was designed to relieve the fundamental loneliness that every human experiences. In your own case, to the degree to which your mate does not meet your needs—spiritually, intellectually, emotionally, and physically—and to the degree to which you do not meet your mate's needs, the two of you are still alone. But this is not according to the plan of God and it can be remedied. His plan is *completeness* for the two of you together.

3) Marriage was planned and decreed to bring happiness, not misery.

"And Adam said, This is now bone of my bones, and flesh of my flesh; she shall be called Woman, because she was taken out of Man" (Genesis 2:23).

Here is the world's first love song! Hebrew experts tell us that Adam was expressing a tremendous excitement, a joyous astonishment. "*At last,* I have someone corresponding to me!" His phrase, "bone of my bones, and flesh of my flesh," became a favorite Old Testament saying to describe an intimate, personal relationship. But the fullness of its meaning belongs to Adam and his bride. Dr. Charles Ryrie makes the interesting suggestion that the Hebrew word for woman, *ishshah*, may come from a root word meaning "to be soft"—an expression, perhaps, of the delightful and novel femininity of woman.

So, when the Lord brought the woman to Adam, the man expressed his feelings in words like these: "I have finally found the one who can complete me, who takes away my loneliness, who will be as dear to me as my own flesh. She is so beautiful! She is perfectly suited to me. She is all I will ever need!"

Can you imagine the emotion that must have flamed within both the man and the woman as they realized what they could mean to each other? Can you grasp the purpose with which God created woman for man? All the tired jokes to the contrary, marriage was designed for our joy, our happiness. And God's purpose has never changed.

4) Marriage must begin with a leaving of all other relationships in order to establish a permanent relationship between one man and one woman.

"Therefore shall a man leave his father and his mother, and shall cleave unto his wife: and they shall be one flesh" (Genesis 2:24).

God gave this three-part commandment at the beginning as He ordained the institution of marriage. It remains the most concise and comprehensive counseling session ever presented on marriage. If you will notice, the words are mostly one-syllable words in the English—plain words, easily understood, in spite of their infinite depth of meaning. These twenty-two words sum up the entire teaching of Scripture on marriage. All else that is said emphasizes or amplifies the three fundamental principles originated here, but never changes them in the slightest. They deserve your careful consideration, for any real problem you face in marriage will come from ignoring some aspect of God's Genesis commandment.

We must understand, first of all, that marriage begins with a *leaving:* leaving all other relationships. The closest relationship outside of marriage is specified here, implying that if it is necessary to leave your father and mother, then certainly all lesser ties must be broken, changed, or left behind.

Of course the bonds of love with parents are lasting ones. But these ties must be changed in character so that the man's full commitment is now to his wife. And the wife's full commitment is now to her husband. The Lord gave the man this commandment, although the principle applies to both husband and wife, because it is up to the man to establish a new household that he will be responsible for. He can no longer be dependent on his father and mother; he can no longer be under their authority, for now he assumes headship of his own family.

Scripture makes it clear that the adult must continue to honor his parents and, now that he is independent, he needs to care for them when necessary and to assume responsibility *for* them rather than responsibility *to* them. (See Matthew 15:3–9 and 1 Timothy 5:4–8.) But a leaving must occur, for neither parents nor any other relationships should come between husband and wife.

This means that you and your mate need to refocus your lives on each other, rather than looking to another individual or group of people to meet your emotional needs. This also means giving other things a lesser priority—your business, your career, your house, your hobbies, your talents, your interests, or even your church work. All must be put into proper perspective. Whatever is important to you in this life should be less important than your marriage.

The wife of a successful businessman who has poured all his energies into his business shed some bitter tears in my office, saying, "He keeps giving me *monetary rewards,* and every time he does it, I think how much better it would be to have his time and love. Dr. Wheat, I don't want all those *things*. I just want him to pay some attention to me."

In more than twenty-five years of counseling I have observed that when a man consistently puts his business or career ahead of his wife, nothing he can buy with money will really please her.

There are many different ways of failing to leave something and thus failing to build a real marriage. I have seen women so involved with their jobs or advanced education that they became more like roommates than wives, and other women whose preoccupation with meticulous housekeeping marred what could have

been good marriages. I have known men who could not leave the
ties with their hunting or golfing buddies long enough to establish
love relationships with their wives. Some cannot even tear themselves away from televised sports long enough to communicate
with their wives. I have observed situations where either husband
or wife became excessively involved in church work to the serious detriment of their marriage. And I have known sad cases
where the mother or sometimes the father gave the children top
priority. When those children grew up, nothing was left. The
marriage was emotionally bankrupt.

The first principle we can learn from Genesis 2:24 is that
marriage means leaving. Unless you are willing to leave all else,
you will never develop the thrilling oneness of relationship that
God intended for every married couple to enjoy.

**5) Marriage requires an inseparable joining of husband
and wife throughout their lifetime.**

"Therefore shall a man leave his father and his mother, *and
shall cleave unto his wife:* and they shall be one flesh" (Genesis
2:24).

The next principle to be learned from this ordinance is that it is
no use leaving unless you are ready to spend a lifetime *cleaving*.
Again, notice that the Lord directs this to the husband especially,
although the principle applies to both partners.

What does it mean to cleave? The word sometimes causes
confusion because in the English it has two opposite definitions
and the most common of these is "to divide," to split, to open."
Thus, butchers use a cleaver to cut meat into various pieces.
Splitting and dividing is precisely *not* what is meant here, so
picture the reverse. "Cleave" (derived from Anglo-Saxon and
Germanic speech) also means: "to adhere, to stick, to be attached
by some strong tie." This verb suggests determined action in its
essential meaning, so there is nothing passive about the act of
cleaving. For example, the word "climb" is said to be closely
akin to "cleave."

The same feeling of action accompanies the Hebrew word

dabaq which the King James Bible translates as "cleave." Here are some definitions of *dabaq:* "To cling to or adhere to, abide fast, cleave fast together, follow close and hard after, be joined together, keep fast, overtake, pursue hard, stick to, take, catch by pursuit." Modern Bible translators usually change "cleave" to "cling to" or "hold fast to." When we come to the Greek New Testament, the word means to cement together—to stick like glue—or to be welded together so that the two cannot be separated without damage to both.

From this, it is obvious that God has a powerful message for both marriage partners and a dynamic course of action laid out for the husband in particular. The husband is primarily responsible to do everything possible and to be all he should be in order to form ties with his wife that will make them inseparable. And the wife must respond to her husband in the same manner. These ties are not like the pretty silken ribbons attached to wedding presents. Instead, they must be forged like steel in the heat of daily life and the pressures of crisis in order to form a union that cannot be severed.

The best way to comprehend the force of meaning in the word "cleave" is to consider how the Holy Spirit has used the word *dabaq* in the Book of Deuteronomy. These four prime examples all speak of cleaving to the living God.

"You shall fear the LORD your God; you shall serve Him and *cling to Him,* and you shall swear by His name (Deuteronomy 10:20 NASB).

". . . to love the LORD your God, to walk in all His ways and *hold fast to Him*" (Deuteronomy 11:22 NASB).

"You shall follow the LORD your God and fear Him; and you shall keep His commandments, listen to His voice, serve Him, and *cling to Him*" (Deuteronomy 13:4 NASB).

". . . by loving the LORD your God, by obeying His voice, and by *holding fast to Him;* for this is your life . . ." (Deuteronomy 30:20 NASB).

This indicates that in the eyes of God cleaving means wholehearted commitment, first of all spiritual, but spilling over into every area of our being, so that the cleaving is also intellectual, emotional, and physical. It means that you will have unceasing opportunity to cleave to your partner even in the smallest details of life. In fact, anything that draws the two of you together and cements your relationship more firmly will be a part of cleaving. Anything that puts distance between you—mentally or physically—should be avoided because it breaks the divine pattern for marriage.

Much of the practical counsel in this book will show you how to cleave to your partner under varying circumstances and in many different ways. However it is expressed, cleaving always involves two characteristics: (1) an unswerving loyalty; (2) an active, pursuing love that will not let go.

If you want to test an action, attitude, word, or decision against the biblical standards of cleaving, ask yourself these questions. Will this draw us closer or drive us apart? Will it build our relationship or tear it down? Will it bring about a positive response or a negative response? Does it express my love and loyalty to my partner or does it reveal my self-centered individualism?

Remember that God's plan for you and your partner is an inseparable union that you bring about as you obey His commandment to cleave to each other.

6) Marriage means oneness in the fullest possible sense, including intimate physical union without shame.

"Therefore shall a man leave his father and his mother, and shall cleave unto his wife: *and they shall be one flesh. And they were both naked, the man and his wife, and were not ashamed*" (Genesis 2:24-25).

We see now that the pattern for marriage that God established at Creation will produce something quite remarkable if it is followed. Two will actually become one. This is more than togetherness! No writer, teacher, or theologian has ever yet explained all that it means for two people to become "one flesh." We only know that it happens!

Several elementary requirements should be noted. For this to take place, the marriage must be *monogamous* (for two people only). At the same time all adultery and promiscuity are ruled out, for, as the Lord Jesus emphasizes in the New Testament, *the two* become one. The Bible graphically portrays the miserable long-term effects of polygamous marriage and the deadly results of adultery. Proverbs 6:32, for instance, says: "The one who commits adultery with a woman is lacking sense; he who would destroy himself does it" (NASB). Certainly none can plead ignorance as an excuse! The marriage must also be *heterosexual*. God made one *woman* for one *man*. The homosexual "marriage" being promoted in some quarters today is a pathetic, squalid distortion of the Creator's plan for holy union between one man and one woman.

Although it goes far deeper than the physical, becoming one flesh involves intimate physical union in sexual intercourse. And this without shame between marriage partners. Shame in marital sex was never imparted by God! Instead, the biblical expression for sexual intercourse between husband and wife is *to know*, an expression of profound dignity. "Adam *knew* Eve his wife; and she conceived . . ." (Genesis 4:1). "Then Joseph . . . took unto him his wife: and *knew* her not until she had brought forth her firstborn son . . ." (Matthew 1:24–25).

This word *know* is the same word used of God's loving, personal knowledge of Abraham in Genesis 18:19: "for I *know* him, that he will command his children and his household after him, and they shall keep the way of the LORD, to do justice and judgment. . . "

Thus, in the divine pattern of marriage, sexual intercourse between husband and wife includes both intimate physical knowledge and a tender, intimate, personal knowledge. So the leaving, cleaving, and knowing each other results in a new identity in which two individuals merge into one—one in mind, heart, body and spirit. This is why divorce has such a devastating effect. Not two people are left, but two fractions of one.

In the New Testament, the Holy Spirit uses the Genesis mys-

tery of becoming one flesh with its dimension of sexual intercourse to picture an even deeper mystery: that of the relationship
between Jesus Christ and His bride, the church. ''For this cause
shall a man leave his father and mother, and shall be joined unto
his wife, and they two shall be one flesh. This is a great mystery:
but I speak concerning Christ and the church'' (Ephesians
5:31–32).

Here is the marriage design as ordained by God at the very
beginning—a love relationship so deep, tender, pure, and intimate that it is patterned after that of Christ for His church. This is
the foundation for the love-life you can experience in your own
marriage, a foundation on which you can safely build.

3

Does the Plan Still Work?

More than one million divorces will split American households this year.

About 75 percent of the family units in this country will need counseling help at some time.

At least 40 percent of all married couples will divorce eventually.

Do these predictions, based on past statistics, mean that the Creator's design for marriage no longer works? We have just been considering the comprehensive marriage ordinance of Genesis 2:24 in all its wonderful wisdom, but we might point out with accuracy that it was given in a world of primeval perfection to innocent people who had not yet tasted the forbidden fruit of sin. Can the Divine pattern for marriage really work outside the Garden of Eden? Or does God take into account how things have changed since then? Has He, in fact, revised His marriage plan to fit prevailing conditions?

This view shows up frequently today as people discuss divorce. Here's how one person expressed it in a letter to the editor of a Christian magazine:

> Just because I married the wrong man for all the wrong reasons, does that mean we should have stayed together to make it "right?" We prayed four years for our feelings to change, for our marriage to change; we saw counselors and went to Marriage Encounter groups. Still we found we disliked each other more and

more. Rather than continue to tear each other down, after five years of marriage, we decided to get a divorce. It was the lesser of two evils; either decision we made would have been painful. I feel guilty, thanks especially to the church's attitude, but I also feel that God understands. . . .

A woman made this comment to me at a Christian marriage seminar: "After all, God gave me a brain. If I see that I have made a mistake by marrying the wrong person, then divorce may well be the answer." Apparently she also felt that God would understand her efforts to redeem an unhappy marriage by eliminating it altogether—like correcting a mistake on an exam paper with a very neat erasure.

We must face this issue squarely. Does God still expect people who live in a sin-filled world to carry out the marriage ordinance given in the perfect environment of the Garden?

The Lord Jesus Christ has answered the question. In Mark 10:2–12, which we will quote, and in the parallel passage in Matthew 19:3–12, Jesus communicates the Divine viewpoint of marriage. As you read His words, you will meet the truth in a pure form, untarnished by the hardness of men's hearts.

> And the Pharisees came to him, and asked him, Is it lawful for a man to put away his wife? tempting him.
>
> And he answered and said unto them, What did Moses command you?
>
> And they said, Moses suffered a man to write a bill of divorcement, and to put her away.
>
> And Jesus answered and said unto them, For the hardness of your heart he wrote you this precept.
>
> But from the beginning of the creation God made them male and female.
>
> For this cause shall a man leave his father and mother, and cleave to his wife;
>
> And they twain shall be one flesh; so then they are no more twain, but one flesh.
>
> What therefore God hath joined together, let not man put asunder.

And in the house his disciples asked him again of the same matter.

And he saith unto them, Whosoever shall put away his wife, and marry another, committeth adultery against her.

And if a woman shall put away her husband, and be married to another, she committeth adultery.

(Mark 10:2–12)

The Pharisees had come to Jesus, hoping to drag him into the stormy controversy surrounding divorce. In that day followers of three different schools of interpretation of Jewish law clashed on the question of acceptable reasons for divorce. Their debate revolved around Deuteronomy 24 where Moses regulated the existing practice of divorce by limiting the cause to uncleanness or indecency of the most serious nature. A careful study of the Old Testament indicates that an act of adultery was not considered legal grounds for divorce. (Numbers 5:11–31 gives specific instructions concerning adultery.) This "uncleanness" or "nakedness" or "indecency" Moses designated as the sole reason for legal divorce usually referred to incest, harlotry, or habitual sexual promiscuity. In the New Testament, Jesus called this uncleanness "fornication." We should note that adultery and fornication are words used distinctively and separately in the New Testament, so that if Jesus had meant to give adultery as the grounds for divorce, He would have said "adultery." Instead, He said, "Whosoever shall put away his wife, *except it be for fornication,* and shall marry another, committeth adultery; and whosoever marrieth her who is put away doth commit adultery" (Matthew 19:9).

Here is how the Jews of Jesus' day variously misinterpreted Moses' statement on divorce. Followers of Shammai claimed that any act of adultery was the uncleanness Moses spoke of. Followers of Hillel defined uncleanness in the widest sense. The wife might burn the soup. That was uncleanness. She might talk too loudly in the home. That was uncleanness. She might appear in public with her head uncovered. Again, uncleanness, if the husband chose to regard it as such. This meant any minor fault could be grounds for divorce. Followers of the most liberal rabbi, Akiba, neatly resolved the matter by asserting that any wife who found no favor in her husband's eyes was unclean and could be put away—a blanket permission to divorce.

Observe that the Pharisees went one step farther and disregarded Moses' exception clause altogether when they questioned Jesus. "Is it lawful for a man to put away his wife *for every cause?*" (Matthew 19:3) they asked. "Is it lawful for a man to put away his wife?" (Mark 10:2).

The way Jesus responded to the Pharisees shows us what our own attitude toward marriage and divorce should be:

(1) He ignored the bickering "religious" authorities of the day and their preoccupation with excuses for divorce.

(2) He focused on the Scriptures as the only real authority.

(3) He went back to the original design of marriage in the Genesis account as the only relevant topic of discussion. Matthew records that Jesus first answered the Pharisees this way: "Haven't you even read Genesis 1:27 and 2:24, you people who are always boasting about your knowledge of the Scriptures?" Or, in other words, "Why don't you go to the original teaching on marriage to find your answers?"

Clearly, Jesus recognized these two Genesis passages as the Divine ordinance for marriage—the first and last word—which remains very much in effect, even in a sin-filled world. Jesus made it clear that the legal concession on divorce given by Moses in Deuteronomy 24:1 simply was not the issue for anyone wanting to understand God's plan and purpose concerning marriage. "He saith unto them, Moses because of the hardness of your hearts suffered you to put away your wives: but from the beginning it was not so" (Matthew 19:8).

From the beginning it was not so! With these words, Jesus directs us back to the beginning where we still find our instruction for marriage and the standards we need to follow. Let us note carefully the one statement that the Son of God adds to the ordinance of Genesis: "What therefore God hath joined together, let not man put asunder" (Matthew 19:6; Mark 10:9).

This adds three important facts to our foundational understanding of marriage:

(1) God Himself has joined husband and wife together. A man and woman marry by their own choice, but when they do so, God yokes them together, changing what has been "two" into "one."

(2) From the Divine viewpoint, marriage is an indissoluble union which all the courts of the land cannot dissolve. How can a piece of paper change what God Himself has done? Only death can part two joined in marriage.

(3) For any individual to *try* to separate what God Himself has joined together is an act of arrogant defiance against the express will of God. Anyone who chooses to do this must live with the results of his action.

To summarize, Jesus told people who were preoccupied with finding excuses for divorce that their emphasis was all wrong. The real issue in the eyes of God then and today is the permanence of marriage and our honoring of this in personal experience.

If any reject these conclusions as hopelessly out of step in today's world, I can only quote the words of the Lord Jesus: "Whosoever therefore shall be ashamed of me and of my words in this adulterous and sinful generation; of him also shall the Son of man be ashamed, when he cometh in the glory of his Father with the holy angels" (Mark 8:38).

Now, how does the issue of divorce relate to your situation? If you are trying to build a love relationship in your marriage, or if you are trying to work out problems in your marriage, even admitting the faintest possibility of divorce will affect your efforts adversely. Retaining the idea of divorce in your emotional vocabulary—even as a last-ditch option—will hinder the total effort you would otherwise pour into your marriage. It will sabotage your attempts to improve your relationship, and an unhappy situation can continue in your home indefinitely. Keeping divorce as an escape clause indicates a flaw in your commitment to each other, even as a tiny crack that can be fatally widened by the many forces working to destroy homes and families.

The gloomy statistics quoted at the beginning of this chapter are due in part to Satan's unceasing attempts to undermine the home, the most valuable institution on earth. They can be attributed to the widely-held idea that if the marriage doesn't work, a divorce should be obtained and another attempt made with a new partner—as we have seen, a totally unbiblical view promoted by the world system under Satan's influence.

Another fundamental cause for marital disharmony exists, and we need to recognize it as we work to develop a real love relationship. I suggest that you thoughtfully read Genesis 3, which describes the failure of man and woman to obey God in an ideal environment; their fall from a state of innocence into sin and death; God's promise of redemption; and the expulsion of the couple from the Garden of Eden to live a life of moral responsibility under new and difficult conditions.

You will find in chapter 3 the origins of sin and shame, of selfishness and self-centeredness and separateness—these all corrupting the magnificent love and unity that Adam and Eve had once enjoyed. Now, in a sense, every couple puts on fig leaves and hides behind trees of their own making! We all have the tendency to withdraw from each other, to be separate, to concentrate on our own needs and wants, to live for ourselves, to blame those closest to us in order to protect or excuse ourselves, and to do that which displeases God.

Sin creates a false hunger, not for communion and fellowship, but for individuality of a destructive nature. Of course, Satan is glad to encourage this tendency. Remember that sin first came on the earthly scene in the first marriage, and in the very first family, division and hatred sprang up. That is where the devil began his deadliest work, and this is why you will never have a strong, happy marriage and a harmonious family life just as a matter of course.

Selfish individuality leading to separateness between husband and wife can be witnessed all around us and is constantly dramatized on television. For example, this dialog between husband and wife appeared on a family television series:

Young husband comes home exuberantly happy with the news that he has a big opportunity to further his professional baseball career by playing in Puerto Rico for a few months. He is excited about taking his bride with him.

Young wife answers coldly: "Why should I want to go to Puerto Rico?"

Husband (just not believing this) stammers: "But . . . but . . . Susan, you're my wife!"

Susan angrily replies: "Yes, but I'm a PERSON too, and I HAVE MY OWN LIFE TO LIVE!"

The aftershock of Genesis 3 is plainly seen in that interchange. Creeping separateness sometimes affects marriages that the public has taken to its heart. Many were saddened to read the newspaper article concerning an Olympic star who became a household word after his remarkable victory. He and his wife had been admired for their united efforts in working together for years to reach that goal. The Associated Press reported that this young man and his wife were legally separating after seven years of marriage because, to quote their public relations spokesman, "the couple feel their lives have changed in the last year and each wishes to focus on his own life." Hopefully, this marriage may still be saved, but note the reason for their separation: so each can focus on his own life! Again, we see the results of Genesis 3.

In chapter 2, I told you about Dean and Carol, a Christian couple who endured all kinds of onslaughts against their marriage, both from within and without. The pressures on them to separate were enormous. Let's analyze some of these and observe how one mistake led to the next. In each instance there was an absence of understanding or a lack of application of the biblical principles that help and heal such situations.

(1) First of all, they had failed to cleave to each other through the years by neglecting their love relationship. A love affair between husband and wife must be kept in constant repair and always on the growing edge.

(2) This left an emotional vacuum that the other woman hap-

pily filled, hoping to separate Dean from his wife so that she could marry him.

(3) Dean's subsequent sin of adultery attacked their one-flesh relationship.

(4) Carol mistakenly opened up her marriage to outside discussion with a friend who constantly criticized Dean, causing Carol to see herself separately from her husband.

(5) This friend also gave unbiblical counsel, urging divorce as a necessity because of adultery.

(6) Carol's physical and emotional withdrawal from her husband during this critical time contributed to the deepening division between them and played into the hands of the other woman who continued to pursue Dean.

(7) The church leaders failed to counsel Dean properly concerning forgiveness and restoration after his open confession of sin to the church board.

(8) As a result, Dean became entrapped by guilt feelings that hindered him from taking the necessary steps toward restoring love and trust in his marriage.

(9) This also affected his ability to go on in Christian growth. Guilt feelings *after confession of sin and repentance* have a satanic origin and are designed to hinder our spiritual growth.

(10) Understandably, Dean felt conspicuous and uncomfortable among the church people who were gossiping about him and criticizing him. He began to stay away from the services.

(11) Some of the church leaders made the mistake of predicting divorce as inevitable for the couple. This brought added confusion to Carol at a time when she needed to hear counsel from God's Word as to how she should meet the situation biblically.

(12) Because Carol failed to forgive her husband and leave the past behind according to biblical principles, they both became almost hopelessly entangled in problems that could have been resolved quickly with proper counseling.

(13) All of these factors, with the emotional pain and confusion involved, prompted Dean to seek escape by moving away, putting physical distance between him and his wife in an effort to

determine whether they still loved each other. Separation seldom enhances a troubled marriage, and it is unlikely to prove anything about love. Togetherness in marriage is biblical. Separateness is satanic. This may sound like an oversimplification, but it is in complete accord with the Scriptures on marriage. I hope you will remember it as a rule to be followed in questionable situations.

Both Dean and Carol found that their feelings were leading them astray, that they could not depend on feelings to guide them. Almost everywhere they turned, they heard the word *divorce*. All the pressures on them urged separation rather than unity. But when they discovered the foundational principle of marriage—that in God's eyes husband and wife are one and must remain one—they were able to restore their love relationship and to rebuild their marriage. Today they have great opportunities to minister to other couples who are going through similar difficulties.

You see, it is possible to reasonably recover the Garden situation in marriage, according to the New Testament. We can, to a great extent, return to the ideal in our relationships, and we must if we want love-filled marriages. Although the tendency to selfishness always exists because of the Fall, we can regain the self-giving love, the oneness, the joyous freedom in communication that Adam and Eve once experienced. Through the resources of the Lord Jesus Christ, Christians have not only the pattern for ideal marriage, but also the purpose to fulfill that pattern, and the power to do it.

We earlier posed the question: Has God revised His marriage plan to fit prevailing conditions in a sin-filled world? The answer, we see, is a resounding NO. On the contrary, He expects us to revise our behavior to fit His standards for marriage *for our own good and blessing*, and He knows, because of the new life offered in Christ, that we can do it.

Of course, I am writing to you at the place where you are now. Whatever your past mistakes in the area of marriage and divorce, ask God's forgiveness and accept it, knowing that you have been set free from guilt. He always deals with us in the now, and you have every opportunity to go forward in a new way, "forgetting what lies behind and reaching forward to what lies ahead" (Philippians 3:13 NASB). With your eyes on Jesus and your mind shaped by the Word, you can make a new life for yourself and your partner from this moment forth.

I trust that you will approach your marriage with a new resolve to overcome the outside influences that cause you to see yourself separately from your mate; with a new determination to do all you can to build a love relationship in keeping with God's plan; and with a new confidence that it will be possible for you to improve your marriage and to remold it in the shape of the original design.

A man once said, "Ideals are like stars; we will not succeed in touching them with our hands, but following them, as the seafaring man on the desert of waters, we will reach our destiny."

We will not achieve perfection in our marriage, but as we follow the God-given pattern of Genesis 2:24, we will discover the thrills and wonders He planned for us, and we will fulfill the purpose He has set before us of showing His love to a needy world through the example of our own love.

4

Love: Solving the Mystery

The couple sitting across the desk from me had come from another part of the United States for counsel. Hal, a good-looking young man, who was already a success in his chosen profession, spoke for both of them. "Dr. Wheat, please help us—*if you can.* We're desperate."

As we talked together for a period of hours, I noticed how seldom Hal looked at his wife, Genie. And she, a pretty blonde with a gentle voice and sweet smile, seemed subdued in his presence. At times I detected a sparkle of warmth in her blue eyes, but it was never directed toward her husband. They were like courteous strangers, not even close enough to be hostile, bound by the most intimate of bonds, and yet farther apart than the walls of my office would allow. In spirit they were on opposite sides of the world!

Yet they appeared to have more than their share of good fortune. They were attractive people, financially comfortable, well-educated, both with professions, and, most important, they knew and loved the Lord. In fact, they had met through a campus ministry, found that they had the same spiritual goals, and decided to marry after a time of prayerful consideration. To an outsider the marriage might have seemed ideal. But I saw before me two acutely unhappy people, struggling just to get through the next week together.

"We thought it was God's will for us to marry," Hal explained bleakly. "We have studied what the Bible teaches about marriage, and we *know* that divorce is not an option for us as Christians. But what are we going to do? We just don't love each other."

Further discussion clarified that statement. The couple respected, even admired, each other as individuals; they certainly wished each other well. But that was the extent of their real involvement. What was lacking?

"Feelings, Dr. Wheat," they both agreed. "We don't have any of the emotions that go with love. It's no thrill being together. We don't feel drawn to touch each other. We can't seem to talk to each other about our past or make any plans for the future.

"We don't fuss, we don't fight," said Hal. "But we don't enjoy each other either."

Any evening spent alone together resulted in boredom. Hal found Genie's sexual responses uninspiring, although they both regularly experienced sexual release. He admitted that he had no desire to sit close to her or put his arm around her. "I wish that I did," he said.

Genie found Hal to be self-occupied and moody. "But he's good in many ways," she said. "Since we both work, he helps me around the house. He takes me anywhere I want to go. He has told me I'm an excellent wife with a good head on my shoulders. And yet I know I don't please him. For instance, he thinks I look terrible without my make-up first thing in the morning. If he loved me, would that make any difference? I've always believed that real love shaded out imperfections."

"Actually, she's too perfect, too nice a person," Hal said. "Maybe that's why I feel there's no way she could ever understand me and the kind of life I led before I became a Christian."

"We're not on the same wavelength," Genie concluded sadly. "Marriage is nothing like I dreamed it would be. I feel disappointed and let down most of the time."

"Maybe we've cheated ourselves," Hal shrugged. "Our best friends love to be with each other. They light up the room when they're together. But it's different with us. I don't know what we can do about it now. We're married and we're miserable. We just don't love each other!''

I hear this complaint frequently. Often the phrase is, "We don't love each other anymore." Or that devastating admission: "My husband (or wife) doesn't love me anymore." But in a surprising number of cases desolate people tell me that they have never loved each other, not even when first married.

As a counselor, I have to deal with the tragic results of loveless marriages. The dearth of love has caused men who are known for their Christian leadership to become involved in adulterous affairs, or their wives to look elsewhere for the love they feel they are missing. In even more distressing cases, things have been done with legal as well as moral consequences that have virtually distroyed the entire family. Without going into details, I can assure you out of extensive counseling experience that men and women have a desperate longing for the emotion of love in their marriage, and that sometimes Christians shock even themselves by what they will do to find a substitute. Of course, a Christian need never be dominated by his feelings—in marriage or in any other aspect of life. But a marriage without good feelings is terribly incomplete, and the many couples I counsel are almost always concerned about the emotion of love and the lack of it in some phase of their relationship.

This is why, from my perspective, it is not enough to write a book on marriage only. I see the need to focus on love in marriage—the full spectrum of love, including the emotional hungers that God has placed within us to be satisfied. We know that love involves an incredible gamut of feelings ranging from thrills to sweet tranquillity. These can be keenly pleasurable and warmly supportive. They give color and texture to married life. They provide us with happiness and a sense of well-being even in the face of outside problems. But the absence of these feelings forms a painful void that cries out to be filled. We must not ignore the emotions of love and the longings they evoke. It is only when we acknowledge them and handle them in a constructive way that they take their proper place in our life to enrich us without dominating us.

Thus, in the real world of marriage, we have to recognize the importance of love with its accompanying emotions. But we also need to sort out the truth concerning love, just as we did when discussing the foundations of marriage. Dreams and myths must be discarded. I would like for you to carefully distinguish between the false and the true in the realm of love. Please ask yourself, Am I now operating on the basis of truth or fallacy in my love life?

An observer can see that nothing is started with such high hopes and shining expectations, yet fails as regularly as romantic love in marriage. The present divorce rate with almost one out of every two marriages openly admitting failure testifies to this. But why does love so often fail? Surely it is because the "lovers" have no clear understanding of what love is and is not; they do not know how to love; and in many cases they have never made the commitment to love. The behavior and responses of the majority of married couples are influenced not by truth, but by their own private supply of misconceptions about love.

Where does this misinformation come from? Fundamentally, God is Love and communicates the truth about love through His Word, the Bible. Satan is anti-love just as he is anti-Christ, and he disseminates ideas that distort and destroy love through the world system that he controls.

There are three main sources of mistaken ideas about love. As we discuss these, you may find it instructive to analyze your own ideas of love and determine their source, where possible.

Jumbled impressions. Each individual has collected a body of jumbled impressions about love, including odd notions picked up here and there, dating back to earliest childhood. Some of these are absorbed from family practices and philosophies. For example, entertainer Zsa Zsa Gabor, a member of the much-married Gabor clan, who herself has been married seven times at this writing, expressed the family philosophy when she told a reporter, "Tiring women are forever asking me why my family and I have had so many husbands. It is not possible for them to understand that you fall in love—but you also fall out of love. When you fall out of love it is better to change partners and remain friends than to stay together and grow to hate each other.''

The jumble of misinformation and vaguely defined impressions that most people have collected explains, in part, why so many prefer to look on love as an inexplicable mystery. Apparently, it is because their own view of love is confused and muddled: love *must* be a mystery! Besides, if love is an irrational thing with all its mysterious excitement, then one can be excused for behaving irrationally in the pursuit of it.

This popular view of love as a mystery not to be tampered with was expressed by Senator William Proxmire when the federal government financed a science foundation grant for research into love. He commented that ''200 million Americans want to leave some things a mystery, and right at the top of those things we don't want to know is why a man falls in love with a woman and vice versa.''

Faulty conclusions based on personal experience. I have found that many people operate on the basis of faulty conclusions drawn from their own experiences with romantic love. Surveys indicate that a good number of people do consider themselves experienced. One sociologist interviewing more than one thousand individuals found that the vast majority had begun with infatuations in their thirteenth year and had one or more ''real love affairs'' by their twenty-fourth year. But these affairs often bring two different sets of misconceptions about love to a collision course, resulting in emotional fallout. The individuals involved are apt to develop a painful wariness toward love or cynicism rather than real wisdom for the future. Personal experience provides sometimes questionable, always limited, data and leads to faulty conclusions that are of no use in building a lasting love relationship.

Flawed reasoning due to cultural influences. There is no way of measuring how many flawed attitudes toward love emerge from our cultural influences: movies, television, advertising in every form, magazines, novels, prevailing attitudes of friends, the words and example of popular celebrities, etc. These could hardly be classed as reliable sources of truth and wisdom, but their subtle and powerful effect on us cannot be denied.

While people are absorbing these erroneous beliefs about love, the scientific/intellectual community is, for the most part, staying out of the field. Someone who checked has said that with rare exceptions most psychoanalytic, psychiatric, and psychological books and textbooks do not have the word *love* in their indexes. Not even the *Encyclopaedia Britannica* carries articles on the subject. But one psychiatrist, recognizing that the need for correct information about love is great, has written, ''Love is sought by every one, everywhere. It is a constant concern; it is in constant demand. Can it be found? We believe so, if it is sufficiently understood and properly pursued. . . .''[1]

Certainly we all need accurate information and clear thinking about what has been called *the most desired and the most elusive emotion*—so desired that marriages without it range from boring to miserable; so elusive that some people spend their entire lifetime looking for it, leaving a trail of broken relationships in their wake.

My purpose in writing this book is to give you the foundational principles and the information you need in order to experience the fullness of love in your own marriage. The Bible is the primary source of our material; in fact, it is the only authoritative, completely accurate sourcebook on love to be found anywhere.

Now as we consider four basic truths that can reshape your attitudes and restructure your approach to love, you must realize this: What you believe about love right now—true or false—is presently doing three things for you. It is (1) affecting your marriage; (2) shaping your behavior and responses to your mate; (3) helping determine your future happiness and emotional well-being. What you believe is that important. How much better to believe the truth!

49

Each of the following principles can help you restore love to your marriage or enrich the love affair you now have with your partner. Each offsets a common misconception of love that may have influenced you in the past. Consider these carefully; then I will show you how they helped the couple introduced at the beginning of this chapter.

1) I can learn what love is from the Word of God. It is rational, not irrational. I can understand love and grow in the understanding of it throughout my lifetime.

Perhaps you have not thought of it in this way, but the entire Bible is a love story that we can learn from—the story of God's unfailing love for an often unlovable human race. It is a pursuing love. Throughout the pages of the Bible we find God wooing, nurturing, caring, doing the best for those He loves, always seeking to draw men, women, boys, and girls to Himself. One verse seems to sum it up: "The LORD hath appeared of old unto me, saying, Yea, I have loved thee with an everlasting love: therefore with loving-kindness have I drawn thee" (Jeremiah 31:3).

The Old Testament tells of the love relationship between the Lord Jehovah and the Israelites, a love often likened to the love of a husband for an erring wife, determined to win her back in spite of her past.

In the New Testament the scope of revelation widens to present a remarkable picture of God's love for all people—a love without limits—as He makes the ultimate sacrifice to bring us into the circle of His eternal caring. We see Him in the form of Jesus, the Man willing to go through death in order to do the best for those He loves. John 3:16 tells us who they are: "For God so loved the *world*, that he gave his only begotten Son, that *whosoever* believeth in him should not perish, but have everlasting life."

If we were to sum up all we can learn about love through a scriptural study of God's dealings with mankind, it might be stated as simply as this: Love is always doing the very best for the object of one's love. This is what love is and what love does, and there is nothing mysterious about that.

But perhaps the motivation for this love is the mystery. What is it that makes us want to do the best for the one we love? The answer, again based on biblical principle, is that love recognizes a unique value in the beloved and chooses to affirm the value of the beloved always. Love is a choice.

Of course there is much more to learn about love from the Scriptures. As we observe the daily life of the Lord Jesus Christ, we can see Him displaying perfect love in every situation. We can learn by example. In Ephesians 5, we find a description of ways in which Jesus Christ shows His love for the church, and these are set before us as the perfect pattern for married love. And 1 Corinthians 13 shows us the nature of love with specific descriptions of how love behaves, especially when tested. We learn that real love is always a choice backed up by action.

So we need not be uninformed concerning love. We can learn from the Word of God, the one accurate source of information about love, what it is and what it does. You and I must understand love in order to build it in our marriage, and this is altogether possible because we have the Scriptures.

2) Love is not easy or simple: it is an art that I must want to learn and pour my life into. I can learn how to love.

This principle corrects a common misconception of love, prevalent particularly among teen-agers who think that love is the simplest thing in the world to understand; that it is easy to love, requiring neither thought nor effort. In other words, no one has to learn about love or even think about it. It's just a matter of doing what comes naturally!

The fact is that love is costly. It requires much from the lover even when the giving is pure joy. If you do what comes naturally you will be wrong almost every time. Love is an art to be learned and a discipline to be maintained. We could compare the art of loving to the art of music or any other disciplined life. In my case, I spent years learning the art of medicine, then learning how to put the theories into practice. Most important, I wanted so much to learn to practice medicine that I was willing to put everything I had into it. Many years later I approached the art of loving my wife in the same manner!

If you want to master the art of loving and want to obtain the rewards of a tremendously happy marriage, you are going to have to learn the principles of building love into your marriage and practice them on a daily basis. Above all, you must want to learn and be willing to pour your very life into it. I can say from experience: it is worth the effort.

How do you learn? Again, the Bible has the information you need. The most concentrated lessons on the art of loving your mate can be found in the Song of Solomon, which we will discuss in chapter 12. But salted throughout the Bible are portions of Scripture that give direct instruction in the art of loving. We will be considering many of these. The real problems of life are not disconnected from the Word of God, and you will find as you go through this counseling manual that the Bible tells you what you need to know to become an expert lover, as a husband or as a wife.

3) Love is an active power that I control by my own will. I am not the helpless slave of love. I can choose to love.

It is important to grasp this principle in light of the propaganda barrage suggesting that love itself is an uncontrollable feeling that comes and goes like a wayward sparrow, landing where it is not wanted and taking off as the mood strikes it. Most of the boy-meets-girl, girl-loses-boy, husband-and-wife-split-up plots of films and television are based on the premise that love is a feeling that just happens. Or else it doesn't happen. Or it happens and then stops happening so that nothing can be done to recapture that feeling, once it goes.

The truth is that love is an active power that you were meant to control by your own will. You are not "just a prisoner of love" as the song goes. If you are a Christian with the love of God shed abroad in your heart, you can intelligently choose to love; you can do what is necessary to restore love to your marriage; and you can refuse to be enslaved by passing emotions.

4) Love is the power that will produce love as I learn to give it rather than strain to attract it.

People today are being taught through the persistence of advertising that they must learn how to be lovable in order to be loved. They are told that they will become more lovable as they choose the proper toothpaste, perfume, shaving cream, shampoo, or deodorant. In fact, the list of products almost guaranteed to bring would-be lovers banging at your door or stopping you on the street is endless. Our media-oriented society measures lovableness by three yardsticks: popularity, sex appeal, and use of the right products.

But God's Word shows the real secret of being lovable and desirable to your marriage partner. It involves learning to give love rather than straining and striving to attract it—a powerful secret that relatively few people know. One word of caution. Many mistakes are made in the name of love. You must learn how to give love in biblical ways that truly will meet your partner's needs and desires. The Bible shows how to love wisely and in reality.

Palm Beach publicist Frank Wright has written hundreds of spontaneous love notes to his wife, some of which have been published in the little book, *Hi Sweetie!* This sample shows how love produces love when it is freely (and wisely) given. The husband writes, "The longer we are married the more I see that happiness in marriage doesn't just happen. Let's always hold hands and tell each other of our love. Let's never take each other for granted. Let's 'give' or 'give in' with a spirit of joy. That's what we have been doing and it works, doesn't it?"

The rest of the note illustrates the fact that the giving of love also produces the romantic emotions of love in full measure. He adds, "I'm just doing some wishful thinking this morning. How about slippin' off after the lunch hour, bags packed, and let's just skip off to some romantic spot for the week-end and keep our destination a secret!"

To summarize:

( ) Real love is not mysterious or irrational.
( ) Real love is not a simple, easy, doing what comes naturally.
( ) Real love is not an uncontrollable feeling.
( ) Real love is not produced by trying to attract it.

( ) I can understand what love is through the Word of God.
( ) I can learn the art of loving.
( ) I can choose to love.
( ) I can produce love by giving it first and giving it wisely.

( ) Love recognizes a unique value in the beloved.
( ) Love chooses to affirm the value of the beloved always.
( ) Love consistently does the best for the beloved.

( ) Love is an active power to be controlled by the will.
( ) Love is always a choice backed up by action.
( ) Love is costly even when the giving is pure joy.

In essence, we have been discussing how *reason* and *feeling* work together in building a love relationship between the husband and wife. While most people consider *feeling* supremely important, I hope you have discovered that what you *think* about love will control your behavior, and that the desired feelings will come as a result of the right thinking and the right actions.

This may sound mechanical and far from romantic, but it is not. Indeed, it points the way to a genuine love affair for you and your mate that should provide enough real thrills and satisfaction to suit even the most romantic individual. When reason is excluded from love's excitements, what results is not love at all but lust, infatuation, or empty sentimentality. And who wants that in his marriage? The Christian, if wise, will build all of his life on the truth. Nowhere is this any more important than in love and marriage.

Hal and Genie, mentioned at the beginning of this chapter, had a sincere desire to build their life on the truth. Yet, as you may have discerned, their chief problem hinged on false ideas about love. In our subsequent talks, Hal admitted that the fault was his, rather than Genie's, although he could not pinpoint the cause. "I suppose it's sin or rebellion or stupidity on my part," Hal said, "because I know I could make Genie fall in love with me if I'd just give her something to respond to. But I feel like Genie is not the right woman, the woman God had for me, and even though I don't believe in divorce, all my fantasies involve another place, another time, another girl."

I asked Hal to take the summary list you have just read concerning biblical principles of love and to measure his own attitudes and actions by the concepts I had explained to him. The results were eye-opening for the young man.

He found that he had some deeply ingrained but faulty ideas about love that dated back to his pre-Christian life and the many romantic affairs he had enjoyed. He still thought of love as a mysterious experience replete with delicious feelings that just came. When he married Genie because she was an outstanding, somewhat sheltered, Christian girl, he expected the thrilling feelings to just come again without any effort on his part. When they did not soon appear, he became resentful and, instead of learning to be a lover, he went from counselor to counselor, trying to find someone who would (magically) get the process started for him. He agreed that although he was an exemplary husband in outward details, he had failed to give his wife what she really needed and desired. He wanted a wife who thrilled him, but he did not want to go through the process that would eventually bring this about. He had never made the choice to love Genie because she was his wife; he had never recognized or affirmed his wife's unique value to him. He had made no attempt to learn the art of loving. Instead, he was waiting for her to inspire the feeling of love in him.

"Even though I didn't realize some of these things before," Hal said, "I did know that I was responsible for Genie just as Christ is for the church. I knew that I was responsible to love her just the way He loves the church. But I was using that 'right woman' bit as an escape clause—really as an excuse for my own self-centeredness. I was kidding myself, because I knew that

God's command in Genesis to leave everything else and cleave to and be one flesh applies to the girl I've married, not to some dream girl I've made up in my mind!''

Hal was ready to do whatever I suggested. Learning the art of loving would involve many details that are contained in the rest of this counseling manual. But he could begin by choosing to love his wife and by deliberately giving of himself to her, trusting that the good feelings would come as he changed his behavior.

''God has a triggering action that will stir up romance in you as you do those things that cause a response of love in her,'' I explained. ''If you learn how to love her biblically and *do it*, in six months the two of you will be deeply in love with each other. Try it and see.''

Hal and Genie have an exciting time ahead as they begin to put into practice those things that fire up a lasting love affair. In your own case, I suggest that you go over the summary list as Hal did. Make a mental checkmark where you agree with the statement. What about the other concepts? Remember, as you believe them, take them as your own, and act on them, you are preparing yourself to make effective use of the practical instruction in the rest of this book.

5

The Five Ways of Loving

The English word *love* has to be one of the most unusual words in our language! It's supposedly packed with meaning, yet it seems inadequate when we really want to say something. (So much so that Edgar Allan Poe wrote, "We loved with a love that was more than love.") The word is overworked. Some dictionaries list as many as twenty-five meanings for love, and we're apt to use them all in our everyday conversation.

Just having the one word for everything leads to confusion and absurd comparisons. For example, we love our lifelong sweetheart. But we also love fried chicken or quiche Lorraine, thus comparing our marriage partner of thirty years to a French cheese pie! We love our parents and our children. But we also love books or football or skiing vacations, apparently putting Mom and Dad on a par with a weekend at Vail, or little Johnny in competition with the Dallas Cowboys. We love freedom, surely a thing more precious than the shiny machine in the driveway. But we *love* that new car; also we love our pet cat and a certain record album we bought last week. Not only do we love Jesus Christ, King of Kings and Lord of Lords, but we "just love Robert Redford"—or Bob Hope. It all adds up to careless talk and, sometimes, fuzzy thought.

The confusion increases when we read books that have love as their theme. One author speaks of love, and we find that he really means sexual attraction. Another apparently is referring to an

57

abstract ideal. Still another writes of romance. And another of intense family loyalties. The fifth author describes an undying friendship in dramatic terms. Evidently each writer has a different relationship in view. Yet they all use the same word to define the relationship—love.

Fortunately, in writing a book about love in marriage, we can call upon the precise language of the Greek New Testament for help. As one expert pointed out, "Greek is a very subtle language, full of delicately modifying words, capable of the finest distinctions of meaning." The Greeks of the New Testament era had at least five words that we can use to distinguish and describe the various aspects of love in marriage.

As I give you these five Greek words and their meaning in marriage, remember that this is not a language exercise, but a practical explanation of what love-life in marriage should be when love is finding its full expression in the relationship.

By the way, there can be no such thing as window shopping here. You cannot pick and choose the kind of love you prefer and discard the others. Each builds on the other. Each has its own special, significant place, as you will find when you begin putting all these loves into practice in your marriage. But if they are quite distinctive, they are also interrelated so that the physical, emotional, and spiritual processes overlap and reinforce each other in the act of loving.

The first facet of love we will consider is suggested by a Greek word that the Bible never calls love. However, it describes a very important aspect of the love affair between husband and wife. This word is *epithumia*, a strong desire of any kind—sometimes good, sometimes bad. It means to set the heart on; long for, rightfully or otherwise; or it can mean to covet. When used in the Bible in a negative way, it is translated lust. When used in a positive way, it is translated *desire*, and this is the meaning we refer to. In marriage, husband and wife should have a strong physical desire for each other that expresses itself in pleasurable sexual lovemaking.

Sex is not the most important aspect of your relationship, but it is a definite indicator of the health of your marriage. If tension exists in other areas of your life, it will usually show up in your sex life. On the other hand, if you have no sexual closeness, your total relationship may be affected as a result. Sometimes your sexual responses are turned off because of various pressures or problems. This is not uncommon and can, in almost every case, be remedied. Even while you are trying to work out other problem areas of your relationship, you can learn physical communication together and experience mutual pleasure in your sex life, so that restoring and building sexual desire becomes an important part of the whole experience of falling in love with your mate. In the happiest of marriages, couples find they can always improve their sexual relationship through added knowledge, greater understanding, and heightened sensitivity to each other. The facet of love known as physical desire should never be ignored in a marriage.

The next aspect of love to be discussed comes from a familiar Greek word that does not appear in the New Testament, although its Hebrew counterpart is used in the Old Testament. I am speaking of *eros*, the love that, more than any other kind, carries with it the idea of romance. We might think of *eros* as totally fleshly because of our English word "erotic," but this is not the case. *Eros* is not always sensual, but it includes the idea of yearning to unite with and the desire to possess the beloved. *Eros* is romantic, passionate, and sentimental. It is often the starting point for marriage, being the kind of love that lovers fall into and write songs and poetry about. It has been called rapture . . . exquisite pleasure . . . strong, sweet, and terrifying because it is so all-absorbing.

Eros has a problem, however. It needs help because it is changeable and cannot last a lifetime all by itself. *Eros* wants to promise that the relationship will last forever, but *Eros* cannot keep that promise alone.

At this point we need to draw a line between foolish temporary infatuations and the true romantic love to be found in a God-designed marriage. Infatuation has been defined as an emotional and fleshly response to false impressions or mere externals of another that have been overvalued or lusted after. By contrast, genuine falling in love is a spiritual, mental, emotional, and physical response to the actual character and total being of another who embodies attributes long sought and admired.

Eros love, when enjoyed in the lasting context of Christian marriage, offers wonderful emotions and personal rewards that are the gift and creation of God Himself. This kind of love is wholly emotional and cannot be summoned at will, but it appears as a sure response when all the other loves of marriage are set in motion. You will experience *eros* love in a rich, mature, particularly joyous form when you have mastered the art of loving. More than any other kind of love, *eros* transforms a mundane black-and-white existence into glorious living technicolor. It is a delightful part of the love-life designed for marriage.

The third love of marriage, characterized by the Greek word *storge*, could be described as a comfortable old-shoe relationship comprised of natural affection and a sense of belonging to each other. This love, referred to several times in the New Testament, is the kind of love shared by parents and children or brothers and sisters; the kind of love Robert Frost described when he called *home* "the place where, when you go there, they have to take you in . . . something you don't have to deserve." *Storge* love in marriage meets the need we all have to belong, to be part of a close-knit circle where people care and give the utmost loyalty to each other. When the world shows itself as a cold, hard place, *storge* offers emotional refuge. The marriage lacking this quality of love is like a house without a roof, where the rains can pour in. But when present, *storge* provides an atmosphere of security in which the other loves of marriage can safely dwell and flourish.

The fourth love of marriage is described by the Greek verb *phileo*, which often appears in the New Testament. We will be using the verb form as a noun in this discussion because it is the more familiar term to readers. *Phileo* cherishes and has tender affection for the beloved, but always expects a response. It is a love of relationship—comradeship, sharing, communication, friendship. While *eros* makes lovers, *phileo* makes dear friends who enjoy closeness and companionship. They share each other's thoughts, feelings, attitudes, plans, and dreams—the most intimate things they would share with no one else. They also share time and interests. Obviously, it takes two for the full enjoyment of *phileo*, but if you are seeking to restore love to your marriage without much cooperation from your partner, you can aim for *phileo* on your part, looking forward to an eventual response when biblical concepts have been put into practice. A marriage without *phileo* will be unsatisfactory, even if there is plenty of passion in the bedroom. A marriage with *phileo* is sure to be interesting and rewarding.

We are moving from the physical to the spiritual in considering the five ways of loving. I have saved the best for last: *agape*, the totally unselfish love that has the capacity to give and keep on giving without expecting in return. *Agape* values and serves in contrast to *phileo*, which cherishes and enjoys. The New Testament often speaks of *agape*, for it was this love that prompted Christ to come to earth as a man on our behalf. God loves all mankind with an *agape* love. In addition, He has *phileo* love for those who are in relationship with Him through Jesus Christ.

Agape love is of particular significance to those of you who right now are trying to save your marriage and to restore the love you lost. Of all the loves, *agape* is the one you can bring into your marriage immediately, because it is exercised as a choice of your will and has no dependence on feelings. It is a love of action, not emotion. It focuses on what you do and say rather than how you feel.

C. S. Lewis showed the difference between *agape* and the natural loves by using the picture of a garden. He described the natural loves as a garden that would soon run to weeds if left alone. This is inevitable because of self-centeredness, willfulness, and the other sins resulting from the Fall. *Agape* love acts as the rakes, hoes, shears, plant food, and weed killer employed by a skilled gardener to keep the garden thriving, orderly, and beautiful. When God planted the garden of our nature and caused the flowering, fruiting loves to grow there, He set our will to tend them, to watch over them and care for them as a wise gardener should. This operation of the will is *agape* love—a knowledgeable and skillful love always concerned with doing what is best for the beloved.

A marriage possessing *agape* love can survive anything! It is *agape* that keeps a marriage going when the natural loves falter and die. In *Gone With the Wind* we have the classic picture of an intense, longlasting, natural love finally ending. The parting scene of Rhett Butler and Scarlett O'Hara has passed into American folklore . . . Rhett Butler forever at the door saying with complete and final indifference, "Frankly, my dear, I don't give a damn!" We may not care for his language, but we all understand what he is saying: that even the strongest natural love has to end eventually when there is no response.

But *agape* love is different. This is one of the most exciting truths in all of Scripture. *Agape* love is plugged into an eternal power source, and it can go on operating when every other kind of love fails. Not only that! It loves, no matter what. No matter how unlovable the other person is, *agape* can keep on flowing. *Agape* is as unconditional as God's love for us. It is a mental attitude based on a deliberate choice of the will, and so you can choose right now to begin to love your mate with an *agape* love, no matter how much indifference or rejection you must face.

This was the experience of a man who contacted me for help after hearing our counseling cassette album. He wrote,

I have really appreciated your teaching on Love-Life about agape love, because that is the only thing that is keeping our relationship going. We talk about the kids, other people, the business, etc., but never about anything personal. Kathy will not allow me to put my arms around her, kiss her, or touch her in any way, at any time of the day. If I buy her personal gifts she will not receive them and if I compliment her, she says, "That's not true" or "You don't really mean that" or some other statement that voids what I was trying to say. We have no sexual contact. I want to have a whole, loving relationship with Kathy, but it's like hitting my head against a brick wall. I keep asking God to help me love her and meet her needs, even though there is no response.

What a graphic picture of *agape* in action, preserving a marriage that otherwise would have disintegrated! This is not the end of the story for Zach and Kathy, thanks to *agape* love.

In following chapters I will give you specific suggestions to follow in developing each of these ways of loving in your own marriage.

But first you need to be confident of this fundamental truth: you are commanded by Scripture to have a love affair with your marriage partner! Let's consider this in biblical perspective.

Genesis shows us that woman was created to fill man's loneliness as his lifelong companion and his beloved. Man was instructed to leave all else, cleave inseparably to his wife, and know her intimately over a lifetime—a process designed to establish a powerful love between husband and wife. Other Old Testament writings give us glimpses of love, romance, and sex in the lives of the patriarchs. Then when we come to the Wisdom Literature of Scripture, the private, intensely personal relationship between husband and wife with its romantic love and sexual delight is brought into full view.

In Psalm 45, designated in the King James Bible as *A Song of Loves*, the writer tells of a royal wedding where the queen is exhorted to consider her husband's fairness of appearance, his honor, integrity, and majesty, and to forget her own people and her father's house. In turn, "So shall the king greatly desire thy beauty." The details of the love affair between a king and his bride are exquisitely described in the Song of Solomon as a pattern for all godly lovers to follow.

But the command to engage in a lifetime love affair with one's mate appears in the Book of Proverbs, that book specializing in practical, down-to-earth discussion of life's daily problems and offering counsel out of the Creator's own wisdom. The Proverbs always show cause and effect: if you do *this* in accord with Divine Wisdom, *this good thing will happen.* But if you do *that* contrary to the will of God and all reasonable behavior, *that unpleasant thing will inevitably occur.* The theme of Proverbs 5 could be summed up as: stay away from the adulteress and always be madly in love with your wife. Here is the heart of the message with its clear commandment. "Let thy fountain be blessed: and rejoice with the wife of thy youth. Let her be as the loving hind and pleasant roe, let her breasts satisfy thee at all times; and be thou ravished always with her love" (Proverbs 5:18-19).

The husband has already been warned to avoid the adulteress because she would destroy him *sexually* (vv. 9-11), *spiritually* (vv. 12-13), and *socially* (v. 14). The same principle applies to the wife, for she will experience the same injury as the natural outcome of adultery.

But now the reward for marital faithfulness appears, and it is a rich one! The wife is pictured, both here and in Song of Solomon, as a cistern, a well, a spring shut up, a fountain sealed for her husband, whose waters will satisfy to the fullest. Even this may be an inadequate description. To be "ravished" in the Hebrew language means to reel and stagger as if intoxicated, to be enraptured and exhilarated. To be "satisfied" is to have your thirst slaked, to take your fill, to be satiated and abundantly saturated with that which pleases.

That this is a physical love affair seems clear in light of the original language that Hebrew scholars term some of the most graphic lines in Scripture. The verse speaks literally of the wife's nipples and then describes them metaphorically as fountains of wine that will keep the husband intoxicated with her love. Observe that this refers to "the wife of thy youth," indicating the lasting quality of the love affair, and that to "rejoice" together was intended to be an integral part of marriage from beginning to end.

But this is also more than a physical love affair. The word used for love (be thou ravished always with her *love*) is *ahavah*, which includes the element of emotional love in response to attraction, although it is not limited to emotion. *Ahavah* actually is the Hebrew counterpart of New Testament *agape* love, the love of the spirit and the will, committed to doing the best for the beloved at all times. So we see, according to this Scripture, that in marriage we must express *agape* love with its spiritual attributes

64

through the emotional and physical channels of our being to satisfy our marriage partner fully. This is no sacrifice, for in doing so we too will be satisfied.

Here we have the love affair commanded by God for every husband and wife—an absorbing, thrilling interchange of mind, body, spirit, and emotions. Clearly, there are compelling reasons for obeying the Bible in the area of marriage! We remain free to resist love and refuse joy, and nothing can prevent us from following that course if we choose to. But we also are free to love, and if we do so in biblical ways, we will experience the blessings of being essentially and habitually *in love*.

Beyond personal blessing, we should realize that God designed marriage to portray the eternal, wonderful love relationship between Jesus Christ and His bride, the church, and that true romantic love is a necessary component of the marriage relationship in order to complete the picture of Christ's love for His people.

It is an exciting fact that when you enter into the marriage designed by God with your love for each other reflecting Christ's love like a mirror for all to see, you also are entering into a personal ministry that will witness to others, enhance all that you do in the name of Christ, and enable you to serve the Lord in a very special way. Not nearly enough biblical counselors are available to aid all the couples needing help in their marriages today, but a husband and wife who have learned to love each other in the ways we have described can minister to a couple in need with great effectiveness.

I recall the time when I had trusted Christ, but my wife had not yet done so. I really searched for some couple who could by their own example show her how wonderful it was to be *in love* and *in Christ* together! We needed such people as friends. As you seek to develop the kind of love-life the Bible describes, remember that it is not only for your pleasure, but it will also become a ministry as you and your partner are sensitive to other couples who need befriending in this manner.

The example you provide for your own children may be the

most rewarding ministry of all. Keep in mind that you are constantly teaching them by example. They will learn about love and marriage (rightly or wrongly) as they observe their father and mother's relationship in the home over a period of time.

A woman, writing a letter to her son and daughter-in-law who were considering divorce, gave them this to think about:

> Your children will feel an insecurity impossible to describe if they cannot count on the love mother has for dad and the love dad has for mother. Children have a right for their parents to love each other. They are their only security. They are the rock or the quicksand under their first steps into adulthood.

As you demonstrate real love for each other and for your children, and as you show them the pattern of biblical marriage working the way God designed it, you will be passing on the gift of love to enrich their marriage and ministry in the years to come.

By now, in light of the biblical concepts we have discussed, I trust that you have the confidence that it is unquestionably God's will for you and your partner to love each other with an absorbing spiritual, emotional, and physical attraction that continues to grow throughout your lifetime together. This means that you can trust Him to work with you and in you as you begin to follow specific counsel on falling in love and staying in love with your mate.

Now I want to show you how you can make each of the five ways of loving a meaningful part of your marriage.

6

How to Love
Your Partner Sexually

When I use the term "love-life," someone usually assumes that I
am going to talk about sex. In our culture, sex and love are often
confused even though they are not interchangeable terms. The
little girl put it into proper perspective when she was being told
the facts of life. "Oh," she said, disappointedly. "I thought you
were going to explain about love! I already know about sex."

Obviously, love is the ingredient that brings meaning and rich
pleasure to sexual activity. Research indicates that out of 168
hours in a week, the average couple seldom spends more than an
hour or two in physical lovemaking. It's what you do with the
entire week that determines the quality of your love-life.

In order to develop a lifetime love affair, however, you and
your partner must maintain a *positive* sexual relationship. The old
Johnny Mercer song comes to mind: *You've got to accentuate the
positive, eliminate the negative, latch on to the affirmative.* . . .
That is what I hope to help you accomplish through the counsel of
this chapter. Even if you already have a good relationship, it can
be better. A mutually fulfilling sex life will enrich your entire
marriage, and it is within your reach!

So let's begin with the affirmative. You have good reason to
anticipate increased sexual pleasure year after year. Some people
dread the loss of their youthful vigor, or they fear their sex life
will become boring and empty through much repetition. But this
need not be the case. People growing together in love find that

67

their sexual relationship provides more meaning and enjoyment all the time. In middle age and later years, overabundant sexual energy can be exchanged for mature, sensitive, skilled lovemaking with a beloved partner whose responses are understood intimately. I urge you to read this chapter with a sense of expectancy concerning the positive sexual relationship you and your mate can enjoy throughout your marriage.

But perhaps you are concerned about negatives in your relationship. If you are to eliminate them, you must first understand them. Physical desire with its sexual expression is without doubt the most complicated aspect of love in marriage. So many potential causes of difficulty exist, and problem solving is complicated by silence, suspicion, anger, hurt, misunderstanding, fear, or guilt, which are often hiding in the shadows. The physiological mechanisms of sexual expression are intricately complex and can be shut down at any stage; yet, when hindrances are removed, they work together smoothly, without conscious effort, to transmit an experience of tremendous thrill leading to fulfillment and complete relaxation.

God's physical design for the one-flesh relationship is amazing! I refer you to our book, *Intended for Pleasure* (Revell, 1977), for a thorough explanation. However, you need to understand this about the sexual experience as it relates to negatives: the entire lovemaking episode involves three phases of physical response that are interlocking but separate and easily distinguishable. They are desire, excitement, and orgasm. To use Dr. Helen Kaplan's metaphor, these three phases have a common generator, but they each have their own separate circuitry. Sexual desire comes from a special neural system in the brain; excitement is indicated physically by the reflex vasodilatation of genital blood vessels; and orgasm depends upon the reflex contractions of certain genital muscles. These two genital reflexes are served by separate reflex centers in the lower spinal cord.

Problems arise when an inhibiting "switch" turns off any one of these physical responses in your system. Leading therapists are trying to determine and treat specific causes of inhibition in each phase. As Dr. Kaplan explains, "One set of causes is likely to 'blow the fuses' of the orgasm circuits, another type of conflict may 'disconnect the erection wires,' while a different group of variables is likely to cause interference in the 'libido circuits' of the brain."[1]

For example, fear and hostility are two chief inhibitors of the desire phase. Sexual anxiety for any of various reasons impairs the excitement phase. Excessive self-consciousness will short-circuit the orgasm phase. This is not meant to be a quick diagnosis of sex problems, but a reminder that your sexual relationship will always mirror the larger context of your life, revealing personal fears and tensions, and almost always serving as a barometer of the total relationship between you and your partner—which can fluctuate, depending on how well you are getting along in other areas of your marriage. Negative feelings in a marriage will often show up first in a couple's sex life.

I saw a couple recently who made an appointment for sex counseling because of the wife's inability to enjoy sex. It became apparent that the real problem was a seething hostility on the wife's part that had little to do with sex technique. In a short time, when the real issue was recognized by both partners and dealt with, the couple reported that their sex life was far better than ever before.

Another man told me, "My wife and I have a good, if not excellent, sex life together. But when other problems come up, we use sex in a negative way against each other." He added with a rueful smile, "You need to give a seminar on how *not* to use sex!"

Ironically, negative feelings are easily vented through the very act that God designed to bring two people together as one flesh. Sex can be used to frustrate, disappoint, reject, or "pay back" the mate when the individual does not even realize what he or she is doing, or what has caused the "turn-off." Often, of course, it is done deliberately.

Sexual problems sometimes reflect your feelings about yourself, or negative attitudes toward sex that you will have to unlearn. Many sexual problems stem from ignorance of basic medical facts and can be remedied easily by proper counsel. Any of these negatives we have mentioned can short-circuit some phase of the sexual response so that desire is inhibited, a physical dysfunction occurs, or orgasm seems hopelessly out of reach. That, in turn, can give rise to a whole new set of negatives that will further trouble the couple's love affair.

This is why I stress that you must aim for a *positive* sexual relationship with your mate. To do this you will need three things: (1) correct medical information; (2) a biblical understanding of sex that dispels false fears and inhibitions; (3) the right personal approach to sexual lovemaking in your own marriage

1) Complete, dependable medical information.

No one should expect to be a natural-born expert! Fortunately, more people today are recognizing the importance of understanding all that God has built into their bodies for sexual delight. My prescription for you is to read our book, *Intended for Pleasure,* or to listen together in the privacy of your own bedroom to our counseling cassette series, *Sex Technique and Sex Problems in Marriage.* These materials contain an enormous amount of medical instruction, explanation, and counsel that cannot be included in this book. For instance, you will learn how to solve the most common sexual problems and precisely how to give your partner sexual release—a necessity. There is a unique advantage in listening to the cassettes together with frequent stops for discussion. It will open your communication lines on this delicate subject, and for most of you this will be better than a session at a sex counselor's office.

You owe it to yourself and your partner to be fully informed. There is no reason why you cannot be a great lover. (I say this to both husband and wife.) Just make sure you know all you need to know. When the aura of mystery is removed from the physical process, you are in a position to understand and resolve the negatives within your sexual relationship.

2) A biblical view of sex.

Most wrong attitudes toward sex are conditioned by early training, but an understanding of God's view of sex that comes directly from the Scriptures can bring freedom to fearful, inhibited individuals. Hebrews 13:4 proclaims the fact that the marriage union is honorable and the *bed* undefiled. The word translated "bed" in the Greek New Testament is actually *coitus*, the word meaning sexual intercourse.

Those Victorians who claimed that sex was something shockingly distasteful that husbands did and wives endured were tragically far from the truth, but they left a legacy of error that is still around. Queen Victoria wrote to her daughter, "The animal side of our nature is to me—too dreadful." There are Victorians of the same mind today who have trained their children (both sons and daughters) to recoil from sex with repugnance or guilt. The result has been acute suffering in marriage for both partners.

One wife in frustration asked me, "How can I help my husband see sex as something *good* . . . that my body is touchable, meant to be seen and enjoyed by him? I know he was brought up to believe that sex was dirty and wrong, something to be ashamed of and done in secret. He's kind and thoughtful. *But I wish he loved me sexually.*"

Another wife told me of the "training" that brought her and her husband to the edge of divorce. She said,

> I knew nothing about sex except that my mother disapproved of it. So I borrowed a medical book from a doctor just before I got married. I couldn't believe what I read! The idea that married couples would do such a thing was so hard to accept that I almost broke off the engagement. But I loved my fiancé very much, so I went ahead with the wedding. I spent my honeymoon trying to avoid sexual contact. When we got back I tried to talk to my mother about it. She couldn't conceal her disgust that her little girl was involved in something as terrible as sex. Then she assured me that most men did expect it, but it would never be any fun for me. For the first several years I tolerated it and pretended to respond quickly so that we could get it over with as fast as possible. After

71

the birth of our baby, I told my husband I did not ever want to have sex again. I still loved him—but not in that way. I hated the thought of sex. He tried to be kind and understanding with me, but the tension and resentment grew between us. The time came when he said it was all over unless I was willing to change. We had tried a counselor once before, and it was an upsetting experience. This time we went to a Christian counselor who began by showing me what the Bible teaches about sex in marriage. I understood enough at the first session to see how far my attitudes were from the truth and to realize that I could trust God to help me change. My husband and I just fell in each other's arms that night and cried and prayed and asked God to help us love each other sexually. It was the beginning of something good. I am learning what sexual fulfillment means, and my husband and I are so much closer.

The Scriptures tell us clearly that the joyous sexual expression of love between husband and wife is God's plan. It is, as the writer of Hebrews emphasizes, *undefiled*, not sinful, not soiled. It is a place of great honor in marriage—the holy of holies where husband and wife meet privately to celebrate their love for each other. It is a time meant to be both holy and intensely enjoyable. Uninformed people have actually considered the Victorian view to be biblical because they think the Bible forbids all earthly pleasures. Certainly not! In fact, the Bible is far more "liberated" concerning sex than untaught people realize. In God's view there is a mutuality of experience between husband and wife. Each has an equal right to the other's body. Each has not only the freedom but also the responsibility to please the other and to be pleased in return.

These basic principles concerning the enjoyment of sex in marriage are found in 1 Corinthians 7:3–5. Bible teachers have called them: the principle of need; the principle of authority; and the principle of habit.

The principle of need. Scripture tells us, not as a suggestion but as a commandment, to meet our mate's sexual needs because we both have these needs. When husband and wife take hold of this concept and begin to do everything they can to meet their partner's need, they are sure to develop an exciting relationship.

The principle of authority. Scripture tells us that when we marry, we actually relinquish the right to our own body, and turn that authority over to our mate. This amazing principle is certainly an indication of the lifetime scope of marriage as God designed it. It applies equally to husband and wife. Obviously, it requires the utmost trust. People should understand this principle before they decide to marry, for on the day they wed, in God's sight, they relinquish the right of control over their own body. We quickly learn that one of the easiest ways to hurt our mate is to withhold our physical affection. But we do not have this right! To put it bluntly, the wife's body now belongs to the husband. The husband's body now belongs to the wife. This means that we must love our mate's body and care for it as our own. Thus, unreasonable demands are totally excluded.

The principle of habit. Scripture tells us that we must not cheat our partner by abstaining from the habit of sex, except by mutual consent for a brief period of time. Why? Because if we break this commandment and *defraud* our partner by withholding habitual sexual lovemaking, we will surely open our marriage to satanic temptations. Our Creator knows this; that is why He tells us to participate actively and regularly in sex with our own mate. This is not a debatable issue, biblically. It is an inherent part of the love-life of marriage.

To apply these principles on sex in the most practical terms, I suggest that you make every effort to provide your mate with a good sexual release as an habitual part of your life together. Specific instruction is available to you through biblically-oriented books such as *Intended for Pleasure* and Tim LaHaye's *The Act of Marriage* (Zondervan, 1976).

3) The right approach.

I suggest that you begin by looking on sex in your marriage as an opportunity for genuine lovemaking (the making or building of love) through giving and receiving in ways that are physically and emotionally satisfying for both of you. Don't worry about fireworks and shooting stars; the thrills will come later when you have learned the highly personalized art of sexual lovemaking. For now, just concentrate on the essentials: physical/emotional closeness and a positive response that may include sexual release.

To develop a real closeness, you will need to view your sex life in the context of your total relationship. A woman at our Love-Life Seminar asked me this question: "What can a Christian wife with a Christian husband do when the husband seems only to want sex and doesn't care about her during the remainder of the day? He forgets her birthday, doesn't care when she has emotional needs, and won't take any spiritual leadership in the family." The lesson is obvious. Sex without signs of love is sure to create resentment, not response, from your partner.

One thing that will always hinder emotional closeness is criticism. You will find it impossible to establish a series of pleasing physical experiences to build on unless you decide to quit criticizing and, instead, begin expressing in the most positive terms your love, your caring, and your desire to please your mate and meet his or her needs. It is not your responsibility to lecture your partner on the biblical commandments we have just discussed, or to insist upon obedience to them. If your mate disappoints you, you must be careful not to say by word or action anything that will make him or her feel like a failure. Even one slip of the tongue can undo weeks of progress, so emphasize your verbal appreciation for your partner. Words are particularly important in this situation. Husband, one sentence of criticism directed at your wife in any area may well drive away the desire she would otherwise feel that day. On the other hand, one sentence of praise and approval (the more specific the better) is going to do wonders for her and for your sense of closeness in the sexual relationship.

Husband, begin showing your wife in other ways that you love her. Give her romantic caresses at times when you are not preparing for sex . . . admiring glances . . . affectionate pats . . . a smile and a wink across the room . . . small attentions that tell her she is a very special person in your sight. Wife, you can do the same for your husband!

74

All of this sets the stage for the sexual experience. It could be called "before foreplay" technique. Researchers tell us that without affectionate pre-foreplay time together, sexual interest tends to wane. So plan with time as your ally in the development of satisfying closeness in sex. It must be relaxed, enjoyable time. In the busyness of American life, you may find it necessary to plan ahead and to set aside special times for each other. Think of it as a date to take place in the privacy of your own bedroom.

Once you are together, the world should be shut out. Have a lock on your bedroom door and use it. Make sure the children are settled for the night and do all you can to prevent interruptions. You should be able to concentrate on each other completely in a relaxed, pleasant, and *romantic* atmosphere. I receive from wives scores of comments similar to this one: "How do I convey to my husband my need for romance and tenderness before the act of making love? It is seldom there, and without it I just don't enjoy sex!"

A recent survey of women's fantasies revealed that they fantasize romance—not just sex—more than anything else, and most often a romantic interlude with their own husband.

Husband, your wife needs a romantic prelude to sexual intercourse. You may not realize how much your wife desires this or what it means to her. Women must be aroused emotionally as well as physically. They enjoy the closeness and intimacy of sex; they enjoy gentle touching and total body caressing done in a meaningful, not mechanical, way. They want their husband to appreciate their entire body, not just to provide some breast or genital fondling as a means of quick arousal.

The physical side of love rests on the human need for close personal contact, especially the need to be touched in a way that expresses warmth, gentleness, softness, and caring. Men have this need for warmth and affection in addition to sexual satisfaction, but they are much less apt than women to admit it or even to be aware of it. Therapists have found that men often misunderstand this need and seek sex when what they really crave is the physical reassurance of loving closeness.

75

Husbands who are preoccupied with physical gratification should know that even for their own maximum enjoyment of sexual release, they need to have at least twenty minutes of sexual arousal beforehand. We sometimes call orgasm a *climax* and it should be just that: the highest point of interest and excitement in a series of happenings. How do you reach the high point? By *climbing* to it. Climax is a Greek word meaning "ladder." You move to a climax with a slow, progressive build-up resulting at the highest point in a sudden, thrilling release—something like a roller-coaster ride with its long, slow climb and then its exciting plunge downward from the peak.

So when you come together take time to wind down from the outside pressures of the day. Take time to build desire. Take time to enjoy physical closeness and sensuousness. Take time to love each other with words. You don't have to worry about saying something clever or original. Your partner will not be bored with the same loving phrases over and over when it's obvious you mean them. Treat yourselves to pleasure!

When couples strive to obtain an orgasm without regard to enjoying their time together, sex becomes work rather than pleasure. Remember that orgasm lasts only a few seconds. Emotional satisfaction and gratification occur during the entire episode. Women tell me that they do not *always* need or desire an orgasm during sexual encounter, but their husbands cannot understand this and feel like failures unless an orgasm always occurs.

A recent study was made of the techniques that wives report as hindrances to their enjoyment of sex. Husbands can use this list to see if there are areas where their technique can be improved.

- The husband's stimulation of his wife during foreplay is mechanical rather than spontaneous.
- The husband is more interested in perfecting physical technique than in achieving emotional intimacy.
- The husband seems overly anxious for his wife to have an orgasm because that reflects upon his success as a lover, instead of simply wanting to please her and give her enjoyment whether it results in orgasm or not.

- The husband fails to provide manual stimulation for his wife to have another orgasm after intercourse, even though she desires it.
- The husband is repetitious and boring in his approach.
- The husband is not sensitive to his wife's preferences.
- The husband seems too deadly serious about sex.

So, husband, if you want to build love in your marriage, you will try to avoid these common mistakes in approach and technique. Concentrate on pleasing your wife rather than anxiously pushing her toward a sexual release. If she thinks you are pressuring her, she will begin to dread the possibility of failure rather than relaxing and surrendering to her own physical response. There is no need for you to ask your wife if she has had a good sexual release. Most women will find the question inhibiting. Simply give your wife manual stimulation for additional release after intercourse. If she does not feel a need for it, she can lovingly let you know. Many women who enjoy manual stimulation are afraid their husband will tire of it just as it is becoming pleasurable. Or they are afraid it is boring to their husband. Let your wife know how much you enjoy giving her pleasure and complete satisfaction. If she believes this, she will feel free to show you what pleases her at a particular time.

By all means, be sensitive to your wife's sexual preferences. It may be difficult for her to state her sexual likes and dislikes directly. If she does manage to communicate them and then they go ignored, she is sure to feel resentful and frustrated.

Finally, don't take the sex relationship so seriously. It will be best if you can establish an easy, comfortable camaraderie in the bedroom with laughter as part of your lovemaking. At times, sex should be lighthearted fun—recreation for husband and wife planned by the Creator.

Ask yourself these questions about your lovemaking. Any *no* answers will suggest areas for improvement:

- Is it positive?
- Is it relaxed?
- Is it pleasant?

- Is it romantic?
- Is it physically satisfying?
- Is it emotionally satisfying?

We have discussed what the wife desires from the relationship. The husband greatly desires *response* from his wife. She can give him this beautiful gift and delight his heart. However, judging from my mail and counseling appointments, many women do not understand how important, both physically and psychologically, the sexual relationship is to their husband. They do not seem to realize that their avoidance of sex or their lack of response will affect their entire marriage in the most negative way. To the indifferent wife I must give this caution: When there is no physical intimacy between you and your husband, whatever emotional and spiritual closeness you have had will tend to fade as well.

This is how one husband expressed the painful feelings resulting from his wife's lack of response. He wrote,

> My wife and I need help. I feel that all our troubles stem from one cause. My wife does not want to have intercourse with me and I cannot accept this. The situation has existed all of our eighteen years of marriage. We currently have relations about once a month. This occurs normally after many days of my frustrating attempts to have her respond. Then it is not a loving affair, but a surrender or duty attitude on her part. I love my wife. She is an outstanding wife, mother, and friend. Except that she does not physically love me. I'm afraid to face up to the fact that maybe my wife just doesn't love *me* and cannot respond to *me*. I have asked myself many times, What are you still married for? I have no answer. I don't know what to do.

We are not speaking now of a wildly passionate response on the part of the wife, but only of a positive response. When a wife responds, she gives an answer by word and action to her husband's lovemaking. It can be gentle, simple, and loving. It may be enthusiastic; it need not be dramatic. But a wife should meet her husband with open arms and a warm acceptance. A lack of response means that you are ignoring one who in some way is reaching out to you, and there is no worse treatment to give to one who cares for you. Indifference is the enemy of love. So I counsel you to respond to your husband in these simple ways, at least (remembering that your varied spontaneous responses will delight him), and to regard sex with him as an opportunity to build more love into your marriage.

Some interesting studies have been done to determine underlying emotional factors that hinder a partner's response. A primary finding indicates that failure in women to attain orgasm is linked to the feeling that the "love object" is not dependable. All the data gathered seems to suggest that orgasmic capacity in woman is often tied to her feeling concerning the dependability of her relationship with her husband. In other words, the highly orgasmic wife feels she can trust her husband; the low responder fears that her husband will let her down. Since she feels she cannot depend on him and may have to stand on her own, she finds it almost impossible to trust him in the sexual act and to relax and let herself go in his arms. Her deep-rooted apprehension robs her of her ability to respond fully to her husband. Further studies indicate that as her anxieties diminish over a span of time, the potential for sexual response is increased.

What does this mean to the husband who longs for his wife to become sexually responsive? If he wants her to respond passionately with a beautiful relaxation and abandon in lovemaking, he needs to give her the absolute security of his love in the context of permanent commitment. When he convinces her that he will not let her down, he will find her becoming increasingly responsive.

One of these studies also showed that the highly orgasmic women had had fathers who were not passive toward them—fathers who strongly cared about them and their well-being. These fathers had not been permissive; instead, they had set standards and well-defined rules for their daughters' protection in their growing-up years.

Obviously, you cannot change the way your wife's father treated her, but you can give her what she may have needed from her father—a strong, loving concern from a man who is leader, protector, and example to her. If she believes you actively care about every detail of her welfare, and if she can respect you as the spiritual leader of your home, the chances are very good indeed that you will see improvement in her sexual responsiveness over a period of time. (That is, if you also treat her as a lover should in your sexual relationship.)

Those of you who are familiar with Ephesians 5, will realize that these scientific findings bear out the counsel God gives to the husband to provide his wife with a permanent, sacrificial love, a protective love, a nourishing, cherishing love. This is not just something you do in order to gain God's approval. It works! It brings about the kind of marriage God wants every husband and wife to enjoy—a marriage that includes keen sexual desire on the part of the woman as well as the man.

What about the husband whose response to his wife is, for some reason, hindered? The wife whose husband is indifferent should answer the following: Do you respect your husband's leadership as a man, as the head of your home, as the father of your children, and as your lover? If you indicate to him by word, action, or attitude that you do not respect him in some area of his life, you will diminish his desire for you. While this is a biblical principle, it also is a principle emphasized by secular experts in the sex-therapy field. When a husband's self-esteem is reduced because he feels his wife does not respect him, their sex life is sure to suffer.

Also consider this: Have you misused your sexual relationship in the past? Have you used sex as a tool of manipulation or as a weapon against your husband? Have you rejected him on a whim? Have you withheld physical favors to get even with him? Have you been dishonest with him, playing games? Have you battered his sexuality through hostility or criticism or ridicule?

You should realize that your husband is psychologically vulnerable to injury in the area of sex just as he is physically vulnerable to injury. If you have damaged his sense of manhood and participated in producing an attitude of failure within him, you will have to start all over again and build him up by your tenderness, your sensitivity, your respect, and your responsiveness.

Although we have been discussing how your total relationship can affect your sexual adjustment, the opposite is also true. A sexual problem sometimes affects your entire marriage in ways that cannot and should not be ignored. It is most often true of marriages where the wife has never (or almost never) enjoyed an orgasm. This threatens the couple's love relationship when it becomes an issue, and a chain reaction of negative emotions occurs.

Here is what usually happens. The wife begins to feel like a failure because no matter how hard she tries, she cannot work up the right physical response. Of course, the harder she tries, the more the natural reflex action of orgasm eludes her. This lowers her self-esteem and her confidence in herself as a woman. She also senses her husband's disapproval or disappointment, and the sex act becomes increasingly painful for her, emotionally. So she begins to avoid sex. If her husband persists, she feels used, and resentment enters the scene. If he tries to woo her with compliments and caresses, she cannot believe he is sincere because of her low self-image. She thinks he has an ulterior motive in being nice to her.

The husband's confidence in himself as a man is shaken first of all by the sense of failure in being unable to bring his wife to sexual release. It is more deeply shaken as she begins to dislike and avoid sex altogether, and he feels that she is no longer interested in *him*. He wonders if she even loves him. Resentment enters in as he begins to feel that she is not trying to find a solution. The wife's rejection evokes tremendous emotions of depression, as the husband does everything he knows to do to adjust to his wife, believing it is going to work, but rejection still comes. A down draft of anger and discouragement says, Why try anymore?

Actually, both are longing for love and the assurance of love from each other and both are inwardly convinced that they are not loved.

Those of you who are in this situation should realize that this is always a couple problem that has built up over a period of time, so you should not count on an immediate solution. Your belief that the situation is hopeless stands between you and the solution. Once the barriers of persistent discouragement, rejection, and sense of failure are gone, skilled sexual stimulus *will* provide sexual release as a natural result. So both of you need to turn away from concentration on those few seconds of sexual climax and learn to enjoy the whole experience of lovemaking with all its warmth and closeness. Orgasm may be the end of the experience, but your goal should be to please each other, to satisfy the emotional need you both have to know that you are loved and accepted exactly as you are.

Right now you should begin to move toward each other through the uncomplicated avenue of physical touching. As your problem developed, you moved apart. So now come together by warm physical contact, by cuddling and snuggling and holding hands just as you did when you were teen-agers. Sit close to each other every time you have the chance. Sleep close to each other. One couple I counseled held their marriage together by choosing to sleep nude in each other's arms while they were still working out other problems. Take the focus off the sex act altogether for awhile and avoid much discussion of your problem. At the same time begin learning *physical* communication as described in *Intended for Pleasure*.

Husband, take positive steps to meet your partner's emotional needs. Your wife longs to be encouraged, built up, and praised. She wants to feel close to you emotionally. This will come as you love her in the way the Bible describes. A husband can always meet his wife's deepest needs by loving her as Christ loves us, and as a wife begins to respond to that love, she is ready to respond sexually.

The husband's love has been compared to a warm coat he wraps around his wife. As long as she feels encircled and sheltered in his love, she can give herself completely to him. In this safety, she can accept herself as a woman and value her femininity. Then she will be able to entrust herself to her husband in the sexual relationship as the bird gives itself to the air or the fish to the water.

We husbands may not be able to fully appreciate the deep longings that influence our wives, but if we love them with the sheltering love that is described in Ephesians 5:28–29 we will see results! Our wives reflect the love or lack of love we have provided.

As you move toward each other physically and emotionally, you should also move closer in the spiritual dimension of marriage. Sharing in warm personal Bible study and prayer together will help prepare the way for sexual fulfillment as a natural result of the spiritual union that is occurring daily. Then you will find that your sexual union can bring you still closer to God, so that you often want to pray together after making love. Love produces love in all directions!

The principles described in this chapter, when reinforced by a practical knowledge of physical technique, will enable you to build love in your marriage through the avenue of sex by establishing a physical/emotional closeness that is good and satisfying. Remember that this sense of closeness develops best in the atmosphere of security and stability. Within this setting you can give each other the opportunity to be beautiful and varied and unpredictable; open and vulnerable and receptive. Try it. If you are afraid to try it because you are afraid you will be hurt, consider this: the risk of pain is always the price of life.

As we consider how to build the other kinds of love in marriage, we will find that all of them will enhance the sexual relationship. As Dr. Kaplan has observed, "Love is the best aphrodisiac discovered so far!"

7

Romantic Love—
The Thrill Factor

At first glance romantic love seems to be a controversial subject. For instance . . .

Some cynics scoff at romantic love as a myth invented by Hollywood.

Some sincere Christians consider romantic love the whipped cream on the sundae of marriage—decorative, but unnecessary. They see this as a lower form of love that husbands and wives should disregard in their search for higher ground.

Some individuals feel uncertain about the value of romantic love because they confuse the genuine article with that frothy substitute known as temporary infatuation.

Some try to suppress all thought of romantic love because they are not experiencing it. Some rationalize, "I don't have it; it must not exist." Others think, "It's not possible in *my* marriage."

In spite of all this, just about everyone inwardly longs for a thrilling love relationship involving oneness, a deep intimacy with another person, joy and optimism, spice and excitement, and that wonderful, euphoric, almost indescribable sensation known as "being in love." Some people say they are "on cloud nine." They mean that they feel energized, motivated, confident to conquer because they know they are loved by their beloved. There is a sense of awe in feeling *chosen* for this blessed state. With it goes a thrill of anticipation in being together. Most important, a fresh sense of purpose sweetens life because the two have found each other and have, as the expression goes, "fallen in love."

This is not overstating the case. As a physician, I have seen that the emotions of romantic love give people a new outlook on life and a sense of well-being. Romantic love is good medicine for fears and anxieties and a low self-image. Psychologists point out that real romantic love has an organizing and constructive effect on our personalities. It brings out the best in us, giving us the will to improve ourselves and to reach for a greater maturity and responsibility. This love enables us to begin to function at our highest level.

Quite honestly, if you are not in love with your marriage partner in this way, you are missing something wonderful, no matter how sincere your commitment to that person may be. Even contentment can be dull and drab in comparison with the joy God planned for you with your marriage partner.

In this chapter we will suggest ways in which you can revitalize your relationship by adding *eros* love to your marriage and learning how to enhance your present love so that it will become more exciting, not less so, as the years go by.

What if you are having serious problems in your marriage? This chapter is for you too. A film advertisement caught my eye recently. I'm not that interested in what Hollywood is producing, but the headline asked a relevant question: **What Do You Do When Everything Between the Two of You Seems Wrong?** The answer: **Fall in Love!**

This may sound far-fetched, but, in reality, it is good counsel for the couple with a troubled marriage. I have seen couples resolve their problems by falling in love. Other biblical counselors report similar results. Anne Kristin Carroll's book, *From the Brink of Divorce*, includes a number of case histories where marriages hung by a thread. In each of these cases the couple preserved their marriage by falling in love. Nouthetic counselor Jay Adams tells of the many couples who come into his office claiming that their situation is hopeless because they don't love each other anymore. His answer is, "I am sorry to hear that. I guess you will have to learn how to love each other." He says that six or eight weeks later they are likely to go out of his office hand in hand, having the feeling as well as the love if they really mean business.[1]

In all of these cases, the couples have applied specific biblical counsel such as that given in this book. But you may be wondering how it is possible, even under the best of circumstances, to evoke that dramatic happening we call *falling in love*. It seems to be mysteriously compounded of moonbeams and magic. It involves physiological reactions such as quickened breathing and a fast-beating heart. It is one of the most vivid personal experiences a human being will ever have. So how can it be developed— particularly within marriage where two people are caught in the realistic grind of daily life?

The answer is that romantic love can be *learned* emotionally. This brings it into the realm of possibility for all who want to experience it in their marriage.

There are two ways to set up the conditions under which this love can be learned. First, by utilizing your own God-given faculty of imaginative thought; second, by providing the right emotional climate for your mate.

Although you will be using mental, imaginative processes, this does not mean you are to force your emotions. Emotions cannot be commanded to appear, but they will come freely when the conditions are right. Begin by choosing to be willing to fall in love with the person you are married to. Falling in love begins in your mind with the choice to *surrender* to the compelling feelings of love (This is in contrast to *agape*, where the choice must be made to give love consistently.) Surrender means vulnerability and the chance of being hurt; but in marriage it also offers the possibility of great happiness.

Men may find it more difficult to make this deliberate choice to fall in love than women do. Researchers claim that although men have the reputation for being matter-of-fact and practical, they are unlikely to let practical considerations guide their love life. Once their romantic feelings have been strongly awakened, they are more apt to be controlled by the emotions of love than their feminine counterparts and less apt to make decisions based on personal advantage. For instance, the king of England could and did abdicate his throne for the woman he loved. But would the lady have given up her crown, had the situation been reversed? A quarter of a century later, Princess Margaret of England, faced with a similar choice, chose her position and gave up the man.

Researchers have found that women are less compulsive and more sensible when it comes to love. They know how to fall in love instinctively and are more willing to try when they see that it is advantageous for them. As one girl said, "If I wasn't in love with a man, but he had all the qualities I wanted—well, I could talk myself into falling in love!"

In a Christian marriage, the advantages of being in love with each other are so obvious that I hope both husband and wife will make this decision. Begin with the willingness to surrender and to let your emotions take you on together. Roadblocks such as anger and unforgiveness will, of course, get in the way of this surrender and must be removed. (See ch. 14 for instructions.) Then you are ready to set up the conditions for romantic love.

Romantic love is a pleasurable learned response to the way your partner looks and feels, to the things your partner says and does, and to the emotional experiences you share. As you consistently think on these favorable things, your response to them becomes ever more strongly imprinted in your mind. You are learning the emotion of love through your thought processes, and it becomes easier to thrill to the sight, sound, and touch of your partner.

Women's Bible teacher, Shirley Rice, tells her students that she would like to inspire in them the same eager anticipation for growth in their love-life with their husbands that they have toward their growth in Christ. Then she shows them how to use their thought life—the faculties of memory and imagination—to build romantic love in their relationships. She says,

> Are you in love with your husband? Not, Do you love him? I know you do. He has been around a long time, and you're used to him. He is the father of your children. But are you in love with

87

him? How long has it been since your heart really squeezed when you looked at him? Look at him through another woman's eyes—he still looks pretty good, doesn't he? Why is it you have forgotten the things that attracted you to him at first? This is an attitude we drift into—we take our men for granted. We complain bitterly about this ourselves because we hate to be taken for granted. But we do this to them. Men are sentimental, more so than women. We weep and express ourselves audibly. Because they don't do it openly does not mean they are not emotional. Your husband needs to be told that you love him, that he is attractive to you. By the grace of God, I want you to start changing your thought pattern. Tomorrow morning, get your eyes off the toaster or the baby bottles long enough to LOOK at him. Don't you see the way his coat fits his shoulders? Look at his hands. Do you remember when just to look at his strong hands made your heart lift? Well, LOOK at him and remember. Then loose your tongue and tell him you love him. Will you ask the Lord to give you a sentimental, romantic, physical, in-love kind of love for your husband? He will do this. His love in us can change the actual physical quality of our love for our husbands.[2]

Husbands need to stop and remember how they felt when they fell in love. One described it this way: "To hold her in my arms against the twilight and be her comrade for ever—this was all I wanted so long as my life should last."[3]

"When a man loves with all his heart he experiences an intensely thrilling sensation," a writer explains. "It has been described as a feeling almost like pain . . . He feels exuberant and light, like walking in clouds. At times he feels fascinated and enchanted with the girl. Along with all of these thrilling and consuming sensations there is a tenderness, a desire to protect and shelter his woman from all harm, danger and difficulty. . . ."[4]

How was it with you when you first fell in love with the girl you married? Or (if you feel that you never were in love) look at her now through another man's eyes. Think about those things that are attractive in her. Love her with a sensitive appreciation and watch her become beautiful as she reflects and radiates the love you have poured out to her.

I am suggesting that both husband and wife must use their imagination to fall in love, renew romantic love, or keep alive the *eros* love they now have. Remember that love must grow or die. Imagination is perhaps the strongest natural power we possess. It furthers the emotions in the same way that illustrations enlarge the impact of a book. It's as if we have movie screens in our minds, and we own the ability to throw pictures on the screen—whatever sort of pictures we choose. We can visualize thrilling, beautiful situations with our mates whenever we want to.

Try it. Select a moment of romantic feeling with your partner from the past, present, or hoped-for future. As you begin to think about that feeling, your imagination goes to work with visual pictures. Your imagination feeds your thoughts, strengthening them immeasurably; then your thoughts intensify your feelings. This is how it works. Imagination is a gift from the Creator to be used for good, to help accomplish His will in a hundred different ways. So build romantic love on your side of the marriage by thinking about your partner, concentrating on positive experiences and pleasures out of the past and then daydreaming, anticipating future pleasure with your mate. The frequency and intensity of these positive, warm, erotic, tender thoughts about your partner, strengthened by the imagination factor, will govern your success in falling in love.

Of course this means that you may have to give up outside attachments and daydreams about someone else if you have substituted another as the object of your affections. Many people who are not in love with their partner begin dreaming about someone else in an attempt to fill the emotional vacuum. Even if it is only in the fantasy stage, you need to forsake it and focus your thoughts on the one you married.

In a book on how to fall *out* of love, a psychologist counsels her patients to practice silent ridicule, microscopically concentrating on the flaws of the other party, even picturing that person in absurd, ridiculous ways, until all respect for that one is gone. This should indicate how important it is, if you want to fall in love, to give up mental criticism of your mate and practice appreciation instead.

To maintain respect for your partner, never allow another person to tear him or her down in your sight. One of Abigail Van Buren's ten commandments for wives says, "Permit no one to tell thee that thou art having a hard time; neither thy mother, thy sister, nor thy neighbor, for the Judge will not hold her guiltless who letteth another disparage her husband." Practice saying good things about your partner to other people. Think about how much your mate means to you and dwell always on the positive side of your partner's character and personality.

While you are doing all that we have just described, you need to provide your mate with the right emotional climate for love to grow in. What do we mean by this? Here's how one man won his bride, as described to me later by her. As you read, remember that these same love-producing practices will work even better in marriage.

> From the night we met somehow we knew God had a special purpose for us. We could hardly keep apart the ten months before we married. He saw to it that we spent a part of every day or evening together. He wrote love letters and sent cards, phoned during the day, and brought special little items to me. He always hugged me when we met. He kissed me passionately and because he spent so much time just talking and listening to me, I fell head over heels in love with him. He was so proud of me he'd show me off to everyone. I felt like I had been brought back from the dead.

Observe all the ways in which this man established a romantic climate and then ask yourself when you last gave your partner this kind of romantic attention.

In *The Fascinating Girl*, Helen Andelin tells how to create romantic situations. These suggestions can be put to good use by a wife seeking to provide a romantic climate for her husband. The best atmospheres include: dim lights; a cozy winter evening before an open fire; sitting out on a porch or patio in spring or summer moonlight; times spent on or near the water, especially at night; strolls through a beautiful garden; walks on mountain trails or in the woods; drives in the hills; a peaceful, homey setting; romantic, intimate resturants; picnic lunches in a quiet park. Whatever you do, keep it just for the two of you. Men seldom become romantic when other people are around.

Either husband or wife can suggest short trips (even just overnight) that become very special. Shared moments can take on significance. Researchers have found that shared emotional arousal is a catalyst in the development of romantic, passionate love. The emotions do not have to be positive ones, but they must be felt in common. For instance, you may experience an exciting moment together or share the glow of success; but you may also be drawn together as you react to the outside threat of danger. This may explain the noticeable increase in romance during the war years. The key factors are these: there must be a shared emotional experience involving intense feeling, resulting in a physiological response, and the receiving of a label approximating love in the minds of both.

A husband described such an experience to me. He and his wife had been contemplating a separation. He said,

> The other night we had a deep talk about our future. We both felt hopeless and didn't know what to do. She began crying and I cried some. It was strange because we ended up hugging each other. I felt like hugging her and she felt like being hugged. All of a sudden there was an exchange of something important. I felt as if she needed me, and I knew I needed her. It was a rare experience that has given us something to build on.

In providing the right emotional climate, do all that you can to avoid boredom even though your life must of necessity consist of routine. Think of your relationship as a continuing love affair and look at every tender, generous, romantic word or act that you bestow on your partner as an investment in pleasurable memories and emotional experiences that can grow and multiply into romantic love.

There are two additional things you can do to provide the right stimulus for the response of romantic love. The first is physical touching—and lots of it. I am not referring to sexual advances, but to the kind of physical closeness that draws very young people into romantic infatuations. This is how young teens fall in love so quickly and intensely. Married couples with monotonous relationships certainly can learn something from this about building the emotion of love. We all have a need to be held, fondled, caressed, and tenderly touched. As we experience this from our marriage partner and give it in return, love itself is exchanged and the resulting sparks kindle a romantic blaze.

Equally important is eye contact. Psychologists have found by controlled experiments that people who are deeply in love with each other do engage in much more eye contact than other couples. As the old song goes, "I only have eyes for you. . . ." This is true of lovers.

Eye contact shows its significance early in life when an infant's eyes begin focusing at about two to four weeks of age. From then on a baby is always searching for another set of eyes to lock on to, and this becomes a necessity. The child's emotions are fed by eye contact. We never outgrow this need, and when a loved one avoids eye contact with us because of disinterest or anger, it can be devastating.

If you practice warm, affectionate, meaningful eye contact with your partner, you will see how enjoyable this is. When your eyes signal romantic interest and emotional arousal, a spiraling response from your partner is likely.

As everyone knows, *eros* love is visually oriented. This indicates that both husband and wife should be as attractive and well-groomed as possible, whenever possible.

You cannot demand that someone else fall in love with you or expect it as a matter of course, not even from your husband or wife. But you *can* set up the conditions whereby your partner will find it easy to love you. Always be mindful of the kind of emotional response you are establishing in your partner's thought patterns by the way you act, by what you do and say, and how you look at love. Remember to send out signals that are pleasant and pleasurable rather than painful or distasteful, for in a sense you are teaching your partner to respond to you all of the time, either positively or negatively. This is yet another reason why you must never even seem judgmental of your mate—not if you want to spark romantic love and keep it aflame.

One of the greatest hindrances to romantic love is the habit (easily fallen into) of nagging. In a Christian family seminar, J. Allan Petersen analyzed the syndrome of nagging in this manner:

> Nagging is basically a woman's weapon used against the man in her marriage. The recurrent irritation of nagging is designed to get the wife what she wants. When her husband surrenders out of exasperation, he secretly hates himself for doing it and then sets his feet a little more so that the next time around she has to nag more than she did before to accomplish the same purpose. This state of affairs continues until finally the woman has formed a habit of nagging, nagging to get what she wants. She really is achieving her selfish purpose at the expense of her marriage. While she obtains personal and immediate satisfaction of her "want," she sacrifices something very valuable in the relationship. The wife who has to obtain by nagging is a self-confessed failure as a wife. She is admitting, "I don't know how to make my husband so pleased with me, so greateful for me, and so proud of me that he will be happy to do something that pleases me." The nagging wife should ask herself, "How much do I really love? What do I know about real love?" Nagging basically is an expression of a selfish independence.

It should be observed that in some marriages where the wife dominates, a husband may resort to habitual nagging. No matter who does it, it effectively stamps out any spark of romantic love and should be avoided!

At the beginning of this chapter we mentioned some controversies surrounding romantic love. Perhaps we can clarify the facts in these cases. If any reader still thinks of romantic love as a myth invented by the film industry, it can be pointed out that, based on biblical, literary, and historical evidence, romantic love has always existed. Researchers conclude, "Despite the assertions of some anthropologists, the phenomenon is neither of recent origin nor restricted to our culture. Although not always thought of as a necessary prelude to marriage, romantic and passionate love has appeared at all times and places."[5] In a cross-cultural study of seventy-five societies made in 1967, romantic love was found to be surprisingly predominant in other societies.[6]

As Christians we can be sure that romantic love is as old as Time itself, for it came into being in the Garden when the first man and woman gazed on each other. We must recognize that it was our Creator who gifted us with the capacity for the intense and passionate emotions required to fall in love. Clearly, God intended for our emotional potential to be fully developed in marriage and to find its fulfillment in oneness with our beloved.

We spoke earlier of some who feel that romantic love in marriage should be downgraded because it is selfish in origin. They judge it to be selfish because it desires a response. These people have overlooked the fact that romantic love is biblical. One entire book of the Bible, the Song of Solomon, has been devoted to the topic of romantic love in marriage, giving us an ideal pattern to follow in our own marriage. As we consider the five ways of loving within marriage, I hope you will remember that all these loves are God-given and represent different aspects, not degrees, of love. None should be scorned or ignored. Every facet of human love between husband and wife cries out for a response and there is nothing wrong with this. *Agape* may be the most selfless of the loves, but it does not hold exclusive rights to a life of giving. Natural loves also involve giving, even sacrificing, for the loved one. Researchers have observed that a significant component of romantic love is the keen desire to work for the beloved's happiness, no matter how much effort is required.

This brings Jacob of the Old Testament to mind—Jacob, the selfish young man, who, nonetheless, fell so deeply in love with Rachel that he worked seven years for a disagreeable father-in-law, then another seven, in order to marry her. The Book of Genesis says that these years of labor "seemed unto him but a few days, for the love he had for her."

"To be in love," wrote the author of *A Severe Mercy*, "is a kind of adoring that turns the lover away from self.''[7] He was describing his own experience in marriage, and lovers will agree with him. In another sense these words can be applied to the compelling emotional love that the believer feels for the Lord Jesus Christ—a love that parallels in many respects the feelings and responses of a husband and wife in love. Theologian Charles Williams wrote that he was "startled to find romantic love an exact correlation and parallel of Christianity.''[8] This reminds us that true romantic love, undergirded by *agape*, and enjoyed in the permanent context of Christian marriage, beautifully portrays the love relationship of Jesus Christ and His church. Thus, the goal of building romantic love in marriage can be a matter of confident prayer, for this is pleasing to the Lord.

Some people may be confused about infatuation vs. true romantic love. Infatuation is based on fantasy; true romantic love has a foundation of strong but tender realism. Infatuation is occupied with externals; real love is a response to the whole person. Infatuation fades with time; love keeps on growing like a living thing. Infatuation demands and takes; love delights in giving.

An important guideline for Christians to follow is that of emotions vs. the standard of the Word of God. If you are infatuated, your emotions will clamor to take complete charge and they probably will do so. In real love, your reason, instructed by biblical concepts, guides your emotions and shapes your relationship according to God's wisdom. Deeper channels are carved for the expression of this love than could ever exist in an infatuation. Within the depths of this relationship, thrills and strong emotions can add a sweet savor to the marriage daily.

If you have felt hopeless concerning the possibility of romantic love in your marriage, you can take heart. Romantic love does exist, and not just for others. I challenge you to put these suggestions to the test.

Although infatuation thrives on novelty, insecurity, and risk, true romantic love flowers in an atmosphere of emotional safety. The next chapter explains how to supply this through the gift of belonging.

95

8

The Gift
of Belonging

Do most people marry for love? Or do the great majority of
couples marry for other reasons? It seems unlikely that anyone
could arrive at an authoritative answer to those questions, but I
have found two secular books that claim to know. Their authors
assert that most people only *think* they are in love; that actually
they are marrying because of other emotions—sex drive, fear,
loneliness, desire to please parents, etc.

The idea of marrying for love, the authors say, is a dangerous
myth. Anyway, they insist, a happy marriage does not require
love or even the practice of the Golden Rule. In place of romance
and love, couples are advised to treat each other with as much
courtesy as they would show a distinguished stranger and to try to
make the marriage workable.

Interestingly, even these books recognize one of the five loves
of marriage. Although they give it no special name, it seems to be
the kind the Greeks called *storge*. The authors of one book say
that the truly loving union is most apt to be found in elderly
couples who have been married for many years, have reared their
children, retired, and now face death together. They have a
realistic attitude toward each other; need each other's companionship; and care about the other's well-being. The writer of the
second book suggests that the couple who married without love
may find it ten, twenty, or thirty years down the line. Her description of the relationship again seems to indicate *storge*, the
natural affection of marriage

But does one need to wait thirty years or have a foot in the door of a senior citizens' home in order to qualify for *storge?* Many of you reading this book are young married couples or even newlyweds. I would like to show you the importance of building this love into your marriage now.

Mike and Nan Lawrence have celebrated their twenty-fifth wedding anniversary. But they developed *storge* love early in their marriage. Here's what it meant to their relationship during what they call the ''rocky years.''

On the way to our June wedding, we thought we had everything going for us. Our friendship was warm, our romantic feelings even warmer, and, as for the fires of passion, they were just waiting for the match! After we settled into married life, the companionship and sexual desire and romantic thrills were still there. But it was all a little less perfect than we had expected because we were such imperfect people. The pink glow of romance hadn't prepared us for that! We weren't Christians then, so we didn't know that *agape* love could glue us together. Fortunately, something else brought us through those first rocky years when wedded bliss almost got buried under the un-bliss. You might call what developed between us a sense of belonging. We had decided right from the start that it was us against the world—two people forming a majority of one. So whatever happened, or however much we clashed in private, we stuck by each other. We were like a brother and sister on the playground. We might scrap with each other, but let an outsider try to horn in and he had to take us both on! If one of us hurt, the other wiped away the tears. We made a habit of believing in each other while our careers got off the ground. We showed each other all the kindness that two impatient young people could be expected to show—and then some more. It really wasn't long until we discovered something stupendous about our relationship: We found out we belonged. We came first with each other, and always would. Because we belonged to each other, no one could spoil our love and togetherness from the outside. Only we could do that, and we weren't about to! It was too good to lose. A lot of people seem to spend their whole life looking for a feeling of belonging. Maybe they don't know that marriage is the best place to find it.

The New Testament commands *storge* love in Romans 12:10, which tells us to "Be kindly affectioned one to another." Other translations say, "Be devoted to one another" or "Love warmly." An ominous condition of the last days, described in 2 Timothy 3, will be the lack of *storge* love. People shall be "without natural affection."

Applying these biblical insights to your marriage relationship specifically, you can see that to treat your own partner without this warm, kind, devoted affection is unnatural. Why? Because you do belong together. *Storge* is the love within a family— whether it be parents and children, brothers and sisters in Christ, or, most personally, the husband and wife bonded together in a practical oneness that has its roots in Genesis 2:24.

Because this is such an unspectacular, down-to-earth form of love in marriage, its importance may be underestimated. As someone has observed, "Familiarity breeds comfort and comfort is like bread—necessary and nourishing, but taken for granted and unexciting."

I suggest to you that this facet of love we call *belonging* is essential to your happiness in marriage. We all need a place we can call home—not just brick and mortar and four walls, but an atmosphere that is secure, where we feel completely comfortable with each other in the sureness that we belong, and that our happiness and well-being are of the utmost importance to our partner. John Powell has captured the essence of this love in one sentence: "We need the heart of another as a home for our hearts."

Do you already have this love in your marriage? Try the following tests:

Wife, how do you react when your husband comes home wearily and tells you he has been demoted or fired from his job? Or even "chewed out" by the boss?

Husband, how do you react when your wife tells you she's cracked up the new car and says tearfully that the accident was all her fault?

Or picture this scene: An evening of contentment in the

living room. Husband watches football on TV while wife crochets and makes an occasional friendly comment (although secretly she has no great interest in the game). Or while he is buried in the technical manuals he brought home from his business, she curls up on the couch with an Agatha Christie mystery. Or they both sit before the fire, unwinding from a hard day, listening to the mellow tones of stereo music, not saying a word, and not needing to. If the husband who has had other things on his mind apologizes for not being good company, the wife answers, "I just enjoy being in the same room with you whether we're talking or not." Could this happen in your home?

Or picture a domestic crisis: Husband stops by the house briefly to discover his wife in a panic. Luncheon guests will be there soon; the dishwasher has leaked soapy water all over the kitchen, and Johnny got sick at school, so she had to go pick him up, and hasn't had time to do the last minute vacuuming. Some husbands might say, "What do you expect me to do about it? I'm in a hurry myself." Or, "Why aren't you better organized?" Or, "Tough luck, Babe," while heading out the door. A husband practiced in *storge* love is going to support his wife by taking a hand in the disaster—mopping the floor or running the vacuum—as well as speaking the words she needs to hear: "Don't worry, Honey; you'll make it." Plus a compliment: "Your table looks great!" And an offer: "Is there anything else I can do for you? I'll check Johnny's temperature again before I leave." Which scene is played out in your home under similar circumstances?

The love of belonging is compounded of many qualities that scarcely can be unraveled from the overall pattern. However, we need to see the qualities separately, if possible, in order to consciously develop this facet of love-life in our marriage. Here are some of the most important elements, but you may think of others to add to the list.

Practical oneness. Husband and wife develop a couple viewpoint. What hurts one hurts the other. What diminishes one harms the other. Personal growth enhances both. Thus, competition is avoided and the petty sniping that sometimes occurs in public as husband and wife try (humorously?) to cut each other down is eliminated.

This oneness developed over a period of time evolves into a couple philosophy in which the personal needs and values of both partners are blended into a common way of life.

Supportive loyalty. One wife told me: "My husband is such a realistic person—he probably sees my faults more clearly than I do. But I know that he is always *for* me, never against me, so he gives me the security and the room I need for personal growth."

Carole Mayhall in *From the Heart of a Woman* shares a lesson she learned concerning loyalty to her husband. She writes,

> Jack was overseas and his letters weren't reaching me regularly. My vivid imagination conjured up all sorts of awful things, not the least of which was, "He just doesn't care that I am here all alone and missing him so. He just doesn't love me the way I love him."
>
> As I was indulging in the world's worst indoor sport—feeling sorry for myself—the Holy Spirit spoke from a freshly memorized verse. "If you love someone you will be loyal to him no matter what the cost. You will always believe in him, always expect the best of him, and always stand your ground in defending him" (1 Corinthians 13:7 LB).

Observe that the combination of practical oneness with supportive loyalty effectively raises the shield against any outside intrusion. A young wife asked me, "What can I do about my mother-in-law's critical attitude toward me? I am so afraid she will persuade her son to agree with her." If this husband loved his wife with the *storge* love we have been describing, she would have no reason to fear her mother-in-law's influence. Or the next door neighbor's subtle interference. Or the predatory woman's activities at the office. A *belonging* love imparts security to the marriage.

Mutual trust. This has been described as "a bond of mutual reliance so deep it is unconscious." The Scriptures say it best: "An excellent wife, who can find? For her worth is far above jewels. The heart of her husband trusts in her, and he will have no lack of gain. She does him good and not evil all the days of her life'' (Proverbs 31:10–12 NASB). The same should be said of the excellent husband. Your wife's heart should be able to trust in you as the one who will always be there when needed, helping and not hurting, because you are her husband and because her happiness and security mean as much to you as your own.

The *expression* of confidence in your mate is important. A wife described the difficult period when her husband's work as technical representative and trouble shooter for a corporation required him to travel to inaccessible parts of the world. It was often impossible to get in touch with him even by telephone when a family crisis occurred at home. She said,

> One thing helped me immeasurably. My husband told me often—and meant it—that he left home with complete confidence in my ability to handle whatever came up. He said he knew that I would always do the best under any circumstances, and he backed it up by never criticizing me for actions taken while he was away. His confidence in me has meant so much. And it's made me love him that much more!

A wife can help her husband by listening, understanding, and sympathizing with his problems; then by communicating her confidence in his ability to solve the problems and remove the obstacles. He does not need mothering or a dose of positive thinking or even advice, sensible though that may be. Instead, he needs reassurance from his wife that she has confidence in him, that she sees him as a man capable of conquering his environment. After that is established, he may ask her for advice and benefit from it.

Emotional refuge. If you feel you must hide your hurts from your partner, something is wrong in your relationship. *Storge* (the sense of belonging) was designed to be the soothing, healing love of marriage. Each partner should be to the other a haven of refuge from the harshness of the outside world. We all need our hurts soothed; we all need sympathy and empathy from the one closest to us. Love should mean a shoulder to cry on. If a husband and wife are available to each other at crisis times and if they offer a caring spirit, they will fulfill an important purpose of the God-designed marriage.

As the Scriptures explain,

> Two are better than one; because they have a good reward for their labour. For if they fall, the one will lift up his fellow: but woe to him that is alone when he falleth; for he hath not another to help him up. Again, if two lie together, then they have heat; but how can one be warm alone? And if one prevail against him, two shall withstand him; and a threefold cord is not quickly broken.
> (Ecclesiastes 4:9–12)

This describes the benefits of *storge* love, but note that the threefold cord is mentioned for its superior strength. The threefold cord of Christian marriage has these powerful strands: love of husband; love of wife; and the loving presence of God Himself.

Comfortable familiarity. This means you enjoy being together If you analyze why you feel pleasantly at ease with each other, you will find kindness a key ingredient in your relationship. You are accustomed to spending time together without quarrels and recriminations, so that you feel *safe* with each other. At the same time, familiarity should never breed discourtesy. The courteous kindness we show our partners should be even greater than courtesy shown to anyone else, because ours is based on personal understanding and concern.

Although the warm affection of *storge* love seems as simple and uncomplicated as the comfort of an old shoe, it takes a measure of time and consistent behavior to build this love in your marriage—time spent in proving to each other that you can be depended on to be loyal, supportive, and kind. In short, that you *can* be depended on.

It is possible to begin developing this love now, even if you have failed in the past. It will require forgiving and forgetting past mistakes. It will necessitate the adoption of a viewpoint such as the Lawrences described in their marriage: a practical decision to be *one* against the world. It must include consistent kindness in your daily behavior, for this is fundamental to the continuance of love.

Because this love, like all the others, can begin with a choice to do what needs to be done in order to develop it, you possess the power to give your partner the wonderful gift of belonging.

At this stage, it does not really matter whether you married for love or for some other reason. Let the psychologists debate their theories. Life is meant to be lived this day. If you have a marriage, it *can* become a place of *homecoming* and you can begin moving toward that goal this day, first by making the choice to love, and then by demonstrating your commitment in daily actions, large and small.

"The passions of love are exciting," Nan Lawrence said, "but it's the shared trust that makes every day of marriage so nice."

⑨

Becoming Best Friends

"Wilt thou have this woman to be thy wife . . . to live with her and *cherish* her?".

"Wilt thou have this man to be thy husband . . . to live with him and *cherish* him?"

These age-old questions put to the two people saying their marriage vows are always answered: "I will!" But what does it mean to *cherish* a marriage partner and how is it to be done?

When we understand the love the Greek New Testament calls (in verb form) *phileo*, we will have the answers, and we will better know how to cherish and become cherished in our own marriage.

Let's consider briefly what the Bible can teach us about *phileo* love. We find that *phileo* is the love one feels for a cherished friend of either sex. Jesus had this love for a disciple: "One of His disciples whom Jesus loved—whom He esteemed and delighted in . . ." (John 13:23 AMPLIFIED).

Peter expressed his *phileo* love for Jesus: "Lord . . . You know that I love You—that I have a deep, instinctive, personal affection for You, as for a close friend . . ." (John 21:17 AMPLIFIED).

Jonathan and David provide an Old Testament example: ". . . the soul of Jonathan was knit with the soul of David and Jonathan loved him as his own soul" (1 Samuel 18:1). Other translations say that Jonathan loved him "as himself" or "as his own life."

God also loves with a *phileo* love: "The Father dearly loves the Son and discloses (shows) to Him everything that He Himself does" (John 5:20 AMPLIFIED).

The Father loves believers in the same personal way: "For the Father Himself tenderly loves you, because you have loved Me, and have believed that I came out from the Father" (John 16:27 AMPLIFIED).

From biblical evidence we can make these additional observations concerning *phileo:*

(1) It is emotional in nature and cannot be commanded, but can be developed.

(2) It is a selective love, based on qualities in another person that one finds admirable, attractive, and appealing. (One loves *because . . .*)

(3) It is fellowship love requiring enjoyable interaction through comradeship and communication. (Two souls knit together . . .)

(4) It is the manifestation of a living, growing relationship between two friends.

This same *phileo* is the cherishing love of marriage. Biblically, older women are commanded to teach younger women how to develop *phileo* love for their husbands: ". . . the older women . . . are to give good counsel and be teachers of what is right and noble, so that they will wisely train the young women . . . to love their husbands . . ." (Titus 2:3–4 AMPLIFIED).

The fond friendship of *phileo* takes on added intensity and enjoyment as part of the multi-faceted love bond of husband and wife. When two people in marriage share themselves—their lives and all that they are—they develop this love of mutual affection, rapport, and comradeship. They delight in each other's company. They care for each other tenderly. They hold each other dear. This is cherishing!

None of the loves of marriage offers more consistent pleasure than *phileo*. Friendship can reach its zenith in marriage because the other loves of the relationship enhance it. The bond is closer, the setting more secure. The camaraderie of best friends who are also lovers seems twice as exciting and doubly precious.

But *phileo* is by no means a sure thing. It cannot be counted on as a built-in benefit of marriage. It does not automatically appear when the vows are said and the rings exchanged.

In fact, as a counselor, I have observed that *phileo* seems strangely absent from many marriages. Through neglect couples have lost the rapport they once had. Others' never bothered to develop it, perhaps because they did not know how. Or, they discounted its importance, leaning more heavily on the romantic and sexual attractions of their relationship.

This letter to *Dear Abby* describes the dismal (and typical) marriage that has dragged on, even for several decades, without *phileo* love:

> Do all marriages go stale after 25 years? Ours has. My husband and I don't seem to have much to talk to each other about anymore. We used to talk about our kids, but now they're grown and gone, we're out of conversations. I have no major complaints, but the old excitement is gone. We watch a lot of television and read, and we do have friends, but when we're alone together, it's pretty dull. We even sleep in separate bedrooms now. Is there some way to recapture that old magic?
>
> (signed)   THE SONG HAS ENDED

The acid-tongued comediennes of the world make a joke of the situation: "My dear, my marriage was so dull that when my husband left me, he was gone two months before I noticed!"

But empty marriages are not so funny, and a lack of *phileo* creates vast spaces of emptiness that couples sometimes take drastic steps to fill. Witness this letter published in the mailbag section of a women's magazine:

> After thirteen years of marriage and two children, my husband and I decided to risk a trial separation. . . . We are allowing each other at least six months separation, dating others and each other, and sharing the bills. If we make it, it will be because we truly want to share each other's lives, not because of habit or established rules.

106

This couple, while trying to remedy their lack of love, seem to be doing everything wrong in the process. How can a revival of courtship competition inspire the genuine love possible only between two adults committed to each other? How can separation enhance sharing when the two things are mutually exclusive?

There is only one way to learn the joy of sharing yourself with another. That is by doing it! *Sharing is the key that unlocks the emotions of phileo love.* This is the fundamental principle to keep in mind as you seek to develop *phileo* to the fullest in your marriage.

Next, consider that *phileo* consists of emotions. Thus, you must establish the right conditions in your relationship to bring the feelings to life. Once evoked, they need to be maintained, again through providing the right conditions.

Remember that *phileo* is the friendship love. The conditions you set up in your marriage must be conducive to friendship. You will need to be sensitive to the basic dynamics determining how friends are made and kept. Of course, these are known by almost everyone through personal experience. It is a matter of applying what you know. Take a creative look at your marriage as a model of friendship—creative because you are seeing the customary in a new way. How can you put the principles that are tried and true to good use in the setting of your own marriage? Picture your partner (potentially, at least) as your best friend. How can you bring this about in fact, applying your general knowledge of friendship to your specific knowledge of your spouse?

Perhaps the saying comes to mind. "To have a friend, you must be one." That is a good place to begin. We have said that *sharing* on all levels is the key. But *togetherness* turns the key in the lock. Consider these three ingredients of friendship and *phileo* love: comradeship, companionship, and communication. Each begins with *com*, the Latin for "together." Comradeship literally means "together in the same chamber or room"; companionship literally means "taking bread together"; communication literally means "possessing together."

107

Clearly, then, the two of you are going to have to plan for togetherness—the kind that involves mutual understanding and enjoyment. You will have to find ways to share meaningful time. And that is just the beginning. "Being a friend" demands conscious effort and commitment. But becoming best friends with your marriage partner can turn out to be one of the most rewarding projects of your lifetime.

It will be helpful for you to consider what some psychologists believe to be the three phases of friendship, adapted here specifically to marriage. You will see that these involve sharing on successively deeper levels. They can be expected to evolve as your relationship progresses. However, you will never graduate and leave one behind for the next. The accomplishments of each phase belong in your marriage permanently. If you want to remember the phases by name, just think of the little red schoolhouse with its three R's. Friendship has three R's too: relaxation, rapport, and revelation.

1) Relaxation

This must take place before closeness develops. It is the time to learn to be comfortable with each other while you practice the basics of friendship. Begin with simple, uncomplicated togetherness. Find things you can do together—side by side. It might be refinishing old furniture or playing tennis or taking French lessons or joining a camera club or whatever interests you. You may want to try something new together. Or one of you may have to make some initial sacrifices in order to find common interests. Whatever you do should provide a meaningful togetherness where you can interact and enjoy each other. Christian couples should choose some service that both can become absorbed in—a home Bible study, perhaps, or a church ministry that can be carried out together. In the busyness of our culture, couples need to give their time in areas that bring them together, not fragment their relationship. If you presently are expending your energies on projects that take you in opposite directions, you should change your projects.

Shared time, shared activities, shared interests, and shared experiences lead to shared feelings and shared confidences. "This was the cream of marriage," Jan Struther said, "this nightly turning out and sharing of the day's pocketful of memories." Andre Maurois defined a happy marriage as "a long conversation that always seems too short."

As all of this takes place in your relationship, you will find yourselves liking the same things, developing similar enthusiasms, and adopting compatible views. Some couples plan private weekend "retreats" every six months where they can formulate short-range plans and long-range goals for their marriages and their families. Fellowship on a daily basis in Bible reading and prayer will give you one mind in Christ, and you will find shared values and ideals strengthening to your friendship.

During this phase you will learn to trust each other—a critical factor in *phileo*. In a survey of more than forty thousand Americans conducted by *Psychology Today*, these qualities were most valued in a friend: (1) the ability to keep confidences; (2) loyalty (3) warmth and affection. These are the qualities you must communicate to each other, and this will lead to a sense of openness between you that draws you into the next phase. As you move into a deeper level of sharing you take with you the growing joy of being together.

Here is a series of statements describing simple friendship. Use these to evaluate the level you and your partner have reached. You should be practicing all of these as a springboard to the rapport phase. This is just the beginning of *phileo* love.

- We spend time together.
- We have fun together.
- We share activities and interests.
- We know and like each other.
- We talk things over.
- We confide in each other.
- We call on each other for help.
- We count on each other's loyalty.

109

2) Rapport

The rapport phase has been reached when you are ready to share aspects of yourself that are precious and vulnerable. Not only are you ready, but it becomes real joy to share yourself with your partner. Craig Massey has defined love as "that deliberate act of giving one's self to another so that the other person constantly receives enjoyment. Love's richest reward comes when the object of love responds to the gift." This is what you begin to experience and when it happens, you don't just *like* to be together anymore. You *love* to be with each other. *Phileo* is well under way!

The rapport phase is a time for sharpening communication skills. The complaint I hear most frequently is from the wife who desires to share her inmost thoughts while the husband feels uncomfortable doing so, usually because he has never found it easy to express himself. Difficulties can be overcome with practice in the rapport phase as couples learn to confide in each other and begin to see how rewarding and fulfilling it can be.

I would like to remind wives, in particular, of five basic rules for communication:

(1) Never repeat to anyone else the things your husband shares with you privately.

(2) Give your husband your total enthusiastic attention and listen with interest while he becomes more comfortable in expressing himself. Remember, it may not be as easy for him.

(3) Do not interrupt him or jump to conclusions about what he is saying.

(4) Acknowledge that you understand even if you disagree, and repeat his thoughts and feelings back to him so that he is sure you understand. Do not let your disagreement sound like disapproval.

(5) When you are sharing your thoughts, be careful never to sound as if you are heaping blame on him. When either of you goes on the defensive, your communication goes too, and rapport must be reestablished.

Husbands should realize that silence presents a negative feedback. As a counselor I have seen how a husband's silence, the seeming indifference to his wife's feelings, and his refusal to discuss things with her can destroy a marriage. It is said, "Adultery slays its thousands, and silence its ten thousands!"

Because women usually feel more need to talk than men, husbands should learn that they can love their wives just by listening. I mean real listening: concentration accompanied by eye contact. Dr. Ross Campbell recommends focused attention as a major means of building love in a relationship. Husband, this means giving your wife your full, undivided attention so that she feels without question that she is completely loved; that she is valuable enough in her own right to warrant your appreciation and regard. Here are some ways to implement focused attention in your marriage:

(1) Spend time together alone—really listening to your wife because you want to understand her better. Of course, this means the television will be turned off!

(2) Look at your wife and move close to her while you are talking.

(3) Plan for times when you will be uninterrupted and then give her the gift of your interested attention.

(4) Arrange longer periods for this so that both of you can warm up, let defenses down that may have been temporarily erected, and feel free to share your inmost selves.

(5) Pay attention to your wife when other people are around. This will mean more to her than you can ever know!

Husbands need this same quality of focused attention from their wives with the personal reassurance that it brings. Through the operation of *phileo*, two separate selves begin to merge and mesh together as you develop a rapport—a harmonious oneness. At the same time this friendship love gives the assurance that you both are unique and valuable individuals. According to the laws of human behavior, this will cause you to become more lovable and even more free to love in return.

Feeling accepted is a necessity in the rapport phase as you learn to share parts of yourself. As someone has observed, "There is great power in being loved by one who does not walk out on you when you are at your worst, or even hold it against you.'' Love may be blind, the proverb says, but friendship closes its eyes!

As you become practiced in rapport love, its joy will sweep you into the most mature phase of friendship where a willingness to learn more about your partner becomes an eagerness to know the beloved completely and to be as close as possible. The movement of *phileo* through these phases could be likened to a wheel rolling along, picking up speed. As the momentum builds, the pleasures of togetherness increase, closeness becomes a way of life, and cherishing your partner is now a reality, not just a wedding promise.

3) Revelation

This is the phase of mature and steadfast understanding. ''I think a man and a woman should choose each other for life,'' J. B. Yeats said, ''for the simple reason that a long life is barely enough for a man and woman to understand each other; and to understand is to love.''

Married partners will agree that understanding each other is a lifelong process. It requires sensitivity, a quality developed as a part of total loving. To be sensitive is to be aware of your lover as a whole person; to recognize your beloved's uniqueness; and to discern what will best meet your mate's needs.

In the revelation phase both partners are freely open to one another. Both have gladly exchanged the original state of independence for an emotional interdependence that is unafraid to lean, to trust, and to seek fulfillment of personal needs and desires. On this level, both the needs and longings of the two personalities are understood and met in a process that becomes almost as natural as breathing.

But a warning must accompany this description of *phileo* love as it consistently matures and deepens in marriage when the conditions are right. A wheel can turn in two directions. If it can roll forward swiftly, it can also roll backward under given conditions, and a backward momentum can occur so unexpectedly that you will be caught by surprise. When a seeming betrayal of trust occurs or personality needs begin to be ignored, a reversal of *phileo* will naturally occur. Remember that *phileo* feeds on response and cannot survive too long without it.

Picture the friendship of your marriage as a fire capable of dying out through indifference. But the fire can be rekindled and its intensity increased until the enjoyment of rapport between you becomes a live thing—like sparks igniting the space you share.

Or picture your friendship as a valuable house. If neglected, it will soon show it. Friendship will fade when neglected. Your relationship may need some repairs, but, like a valuable house, restoration can take place if you care to invest the time and attention.

Always remember that friendship requires attention. It must have something to feed on and respond to. Ask yourself and your partner: What are we overlooking that could make our relationship better? If we are a bit bored, what are we doing to add zest to our friendship?

Any marriage can benefit from more *phileo*. Since this friendship is a living entity, it must constantly grow or it will begin to wither. So think of tangible things you can do to help it grow.

I find it interesting to hear from couples actively engaged in building *phileo* together because they go about it in so many different ways. For Paul and Olivia it meant blueberries and a baby!

This couple had found real unity in their marriage, particularly in the joy of Christian ministry and spiritual growth. But they were still aware of emotional distance. Paul was not affectionate by nature. Olivia was reticent about expressing her needs. They became conscious of living in two separate worlds: Paul in his schoolroom and Olivia in her home. He coped with young people all day, while she developed her skills as a full-time homemaker and mother. At night there seemed to be little meaningful conversation. After eight hours of interaction with students, Paul said that he felt too tired to talk. Finally he told his wife, "You couldn't understand my day, and I don't feel up to explaining what goes on by the time I get home." When they faced this problem, they found a solution: Olivia came to school for visits and observed Paul's world. A deeper understanding developed.

Then they decided to begin a project together—a blueberry patch with moneymaking potential. The real bonus, however, was the long hours spent together over the bushes—row by row—providing plenty of opportunity for leisurely conversation while they learned the pleasure of working together. Paul says now that weeding time just means more time he gets to spend talking with Olivia!

The most exciting project for this couple, however, has been the coming of their third baby—an arrival planned with delight from the beginning. Paul and Olivia decided that this time they would totally share in the delivery through prepared childbirth training. "Before, with the other children, it had been an anxious time for me," Olivia explained. "But this became an adventure. Paul was enthused about doing the whole thing with me. He even studied what foods would be best for me to eat. He put so much time and effort into learning with me—attending classes, spending time on the exercises with me—it meant a lot to me emotionally. Especially because childbirth is such an emotional happening, and we were in this together."

"It brought us together in every way," Paul said. "My job was to massage her when the contractions came, keep her relaxed, talk to her, and become sensitive to what she was feeling. We practiced this long before the time of delivery. It taught me the importance of physical touching in a non-sexual way. As I learned to touch her with a gentle, caring touch, I saw a real response, and I *knew* that my touch comforted her."

"We had been married eleven years," Olivia said, "but we had never been as close. I think for the first time Paul realized just how much I needed him. I had never felt free to show him before. Now I am sure that I am cherished and I can express my needs because of the way he demonstrated his loving care for me all during those nine months—and ever since!"

"As I worked with her, I did become much more sensitive to her," Paul said. "As Olivia realized this, she began to trust me more and this has continued since the birth of our baby. It's part of us now."

"We developed a new admiration for each other through this experience," Olivia added. "And a new confidence in the other's ability to cope with the situations of life. I was so impressed with Paul's care and concern, and his wisdom and sensitivity. And he was impressed with my ability to deliver our baby in a natural, wonderful way. The three of us were able to come home from the hospital the same day. When we got home we couldn't believe we had done it so easily! We accomplished it *together*. What a beautiful feeling!"

Paul summed it up: "We're much more *one person* now."

One of the most interesting examples of the development of *phileo* love can be found in the marriage of Anne and Charles Lindbergh. It is well worth considering because of what it illustrates about friendship in marriage.

The world called it a storybook romance—the ambassador's daughter and the famed "Lone Eagle." But the shy, introspective girl who would marry aviation hero Charles Lindbergh saw it another way: she, "the youngest, most self-conscious adolescent that ever lived" and he, like "a bomb dropped into our college-bred, forever book-reading family."[1]

The sheltered young poet and the man of whirlwind action. He was always in the public eye, his mind fastened on the scientific rather than the poetic—could such radical differences between them be overcome in marriage? Anne Morrow, admittedly "very much in love," recognized their differences in background, training, personality, interests, and way of life, and she tried to draw back.

To one sister she wrote, "I . . . think dazedly, Who *is* this man anyway? I can't *really* like him. It is a dream and a mistake. We are utterly opposed."

To her other sister she wrote, "I am completely turned upside down, completely overwhelmed, completely upset. He is the biggest, most absorbing person I've ever met, and he doesn't seem to touch my life anywhere, really."[2]

When the decision to marry was made, she wrote a friend with painful honesty:

> Apparently I am going to marry Charles Lindbergh. It must seem hysterically funny to you as it did to me, when I consider my opinions on marriage. "A safe marriage," "things in common," "liking the same things," "a quiet life," etc. All those things which I am apparently going against. . . . It must be fatal to decide on the kind of man you *don't* want to marry and the kind of life you *don't* want to lead. You determinedly turn your back on it, set out in the opposite direction—and come bang up against it, in true *Alice in the Looking Glass* fashion. And there he is—darn it all—the great Western strongman-open-spaces type and a life of relentless action. But . . . what am I going to do about it? After all, there he is and I've got to go.

She added, "Don't wish me happiness—I don't expect to be happy, but it's gotten beyond that, somehow. Wish me courage and strength and a sense of humor—I will need them all."[3]

And so the writer and the aviator set out to develop the comradeship, communication, and togetherness that would make them best friends and loyal lovers through almost fifty years of living—years full of ordinary happiness as well as triumph, tragedy, controversy, and accomplishment.

The published diaries and letters of Anne Morrow Lindbergh reveal the intense effort given to melding two such individualists into a deep, close union. The greater effort seemingly was made by her, even as the Bible counsels throughout the New Testament: Wives, adapt yourselves to your husbands.

Anne's adaptation involved learning navigation, radio, and aerial photography—even becoming a skilled pilot herself; hiding her fear on their hazardous pioneer missions; traveling without a settled home for the first years; and coping with endless crowds in the constant glare of publicity. Charles' contributions to the process of developing their close relationship, if less obvious, were substantial and abiding.

116

Most significant for us, this couple proved that *phileo* love can be developed between two dissimilar people even under extreme conditions when the two care enough to pour their lives into it.

Cherishing! It never happens quickly. As the middle-aged couple with six children said, "Love is what you've been through with somebody." But two of you cooperating can bring this cherishing about, slowly, beautifully, like the unfolding of a flower.

10

The Agape Way

But, Dr. Wheat, what do you do about a marriage that isn't *emotionally real?''* The wife posing that question had good reason to ask. Barbara, who at age thirty is as lovely as any model, spends her days at home with two young children while her husband, a high-living executive, crisscrosses the continent on business (and pleasure), often accompanied by his mistress.

I think of many others committed to emotionally barren marriages that are devoid of the wonderful feelings of love we have been describing. Not much friendship or affectionate belonging or physical, romantic love in these marriages! Not presently.

I am reminded of Eric, whose wife, caught up in the sophisticated trappings of a new job, thinks she no longer wants what he can offer her and demands a divorce. . . .

Of Fran, whose husband pours all his affection and attention on his thoroughbred horses and tells her to ''go find a hobby''. . . .

Of Quentin, whose wife has exhibited a sudden personality change and after an episode leading to her arrest refuses to come home. . . .

Of Iris, who has to stand alone in rearing the children, maintaining the home, and coping with finances, ''all without a word of approval, encouragement, or even a love pat'' from her husband, a brilliant but self-centered scientist.

Of John, whose wife coldly rejects him as friend and lover. . . .

And of Una, whose husband has been spending most of his free time at home in an alcoholic stupor. . . .

What is the answer for these people and for others who have no reason to *feel* love for their marriage partners?

God has provided a remarkable solution: a love directed and fueled, not by the emotions, but by the will. Out of His own mighty nature, God supplies the resources for this love, and they are available to any life connected with His by faith in Jesus Christ: ". . . God's love has been poured out in our hearts through the Holy Spirit Who has been given to us" (Romans 5:5 AMPLIFIED). This is the *agape* love of the New Testament—unconditional, unchanging, inexhaustible, generous beyond measure, and most wonderfully kind!

No book on the love-life of husband and wife can be complete without a consideration of *agape*. Even in the best of marriages, unlovable traits show up in both partners. And in every marriage, sooner or later, a need arises that can be met only by unconditional love. *Agape* is the answer for all the woundings of marriage. This love has the capacity to persist in the face of rejection and continue on when there is no response at all. It can leap over walls that would stop any human love cold. It is never deflected by unlovable behavior and gives gladly to the undeserving without totalling the cost. It heals and blesses in unpretentious, practical ways, for it is always realistically involved in the details of ordinary life. To the relationship of husband and wife, which would otherwise lie at the mercy of fluctuating emotions and human upheavals, *agape* imparts stability and a permanence that is rooted in the Eternal. Agape is the Divine solution for marriages populated by imperfect human beings!

Two verses among hundreds in the New Testament will suffice to illustrate the nature of *agape* love:

"For God so loved the world, that he gave his only begotten Son, that whosoever believeth in him should not perish, but have everlasting life" (John 3:16).

"But God commendeth his love toward us, in that, while we were yet sinners, Christ died for us" (Romans 5:8).

We can make these observations concerning *agape:*

(1) *Agape* love means action, not just a benign attitude.

(2) *Agape* love means involvement, not a comfortable detachment from the needs of others.

(3) *Agape* love means unconditionally loving the unlovable, the undeserving, and the unresponsive.

(4) *Agape* love means permanent commitment to the object of one's love.

(5) *Agape* love means constructive, purposeful giving based not on blind sentimentality but on knowledge: the knowledge of what is best for the beloved.

(6) *Agape* love means consistency of behavior showing an ever-present concern for the beloved's highest good.

(7) *Agape* love is the chief means and the best way of blessing your partner and your marriage.

Let me illustrate with a case history—the most beautiful example of *agape* love that I have observed personally.

In this case a man loved his wife tenderly and steadfastly for a total of fifteen years without any responding love on her part. There could be no response, for she had developed cerebral arteriosclerosis, the chronic brain syndrome.

At the onset of the disease she was a pretty, vivacious lady of sixty who looked at least ten years younger. In the beginning she experienced intermittent times of confusion. For instance, she would drive to Little Rock, then find herself at an intersection without knowing where she was, or why, or how to get back home. A former schoolteacher, she had enjoyed driving her own car for many years. But finally her husband had to take away her car keys for her safety.

As the disease progressed, she gradually lost all her mental faculties and did not even recognize her husband. He took care of her at home by himself for the first five years. During that time he often took her for visits, she looking her prettiest although she had no idea of where she was, and he proudly displaying her as his wife, introducing her to everyone, even though her remarks were apt to be inappropriate to the conversation. He never made an apology for her; he never indicated that there was anything wrong with what she had just said. He always treated her with the utmost courtesy. He showered her with love and attention, no matter what she said or did.

The time came when the doctors said she had to go into a nursing home for intensive care. She lived there for ten years (part of that time bedfast with arthritis) and he was with her daily. As long as she was able to sit up, he took her for a drive each afternoon—out to their farm, or downtown, or to visit the family—never in any way embarrassed that she was so far out of touch. He never made a negative comment about her. He did not begrudge the large amount of money required to keep her in the home all those years, never even hinted that it might be a problem. In fact, he never complained about any detail of her care throughout the long illness. He always obtained the best for her and did the best for her.

This man was loyal, always true to his wife, even though his love had no response for fifteen years. This is *agape*, not in theory, but in practice!

I can speak of this case with intimate knowledge, for these people were my own wonderful parents. What my father taught me about *agape* love through his example I can never forget.

Now I would like for you to apply the principles of *agape* love to your own marital situation. Remember that *agape* gives the very best to the one you love. In your own marriage, your partner needs one thing from you above all else: *unconditional love!* Christian therapists speak of "the almost unbelievable need for *agape*." Psychiatrist Ross Campbell points out that there is no substitute for the incomparable emotional well-being that comes from feeling loved and accepted, completely and unconditionally.

You will both experience tremendous benefits when unconditional love becomes a part of your marriage. First, your partner's self-image will be greatly enhanced. The better a person feels about himself, the better he is able to function in a marriage relationship. One who feels loved all of the time, knowing it is not based on his performance but on his unique value as a person, is going to be able to relax and love generously in return. The person who *feels* lovable can express all the loves of marriage. The person who feels he has something to give will gladly give it. Your partner will feel at ease with himself and, as a result, will become a more enjoyable companion.

Second, this habit of unconditional love can carry your partner safely through periods of severe stress. At times when our mates are most vulnerable to hurt because of stress, they are apt to behave in unattractive ways. That is the signal that we need to give more love than ever. Unconditional love will meet your mate's needs during the troubled periods that come to almost everyone at some time. Designed by the wisdom of God, *agape* is the best medicine for mental health.

Third, in an atmosphere of unchanging love, the two of you can find the security and stability that will help you to grow and become the individuals you want to be. The writer of Psalm 52 illustrates this when he begins by affirming that "The goodness of God endures continually" and concludes by describing himself as a green olive tree in the house of God, trusting in the mercy of God forever—planted, rooted, living, and growing. Unconditional love does this for us.

Fourth, unconditional love makes every day a smoother experience, even the most trying of days. Because you have established the habit of expressing *agape*, you do not behave disagreeably just because you are feeling depressed, worried, ill, or fatigued. You continue to treat your mate with courtesy and kindness, and you avoid those uncontrolled outbursts that can be devastating to the love-life of marriage. Because you are practiced, you know how to draw on the Divine supply of patience. Therefore your partner does not become your emotional football because you consistently behave with love, no matter how you feel.

Fifth, unconditional love removes the spirit of defensiveness on both sides. Thus, you do not feel the need to defend yourself from attack or to cut the other down by criticism. The syndrome of incessant complaining and explaining is happily absent from your home.

Unconditional love means that we can love our mates even in the face of extremely unlovable behavior. It means, for instance, that a husband can go out looking for his wife when she has run away from him to become a prostitute. He can find her in the gutter (literally) and take her home to love her back to health and restore her to a place of honor. Does that sound too drastic? Too improbable? A husband named Hosea loved his wife with unconditional love, and their story had a happy ending. You can read it in the Old Testament and in chapter 15 of this book, where it appears in a dramatic narrative form. But this still happens today. In my counseling I have encountered several Hoseas—both men and women—who exhibited this pursuing, unconditional love for their mates.

It is important for you to stop and evaluate your own approach to love. Do you presently love with conditional love? Or unconditional love? Try to answer these questions honestly:

- Is my treatment of other people usually based on their behavior?
- Does my partner's performance determine the degree of love I give him or her?
- Do I think that love should be shown only as a reward for good behavior?
- Do I feel that my partner has to change before I can love him or her *more?*
- Do I think I can improve my partner's behavior by withholding love?
- Am I reacting to other people most of the time?

As you may be aware, people who constantly react are never really free. Someone else is always in control, determining how they will feel and behave.

Your attitude toward unconditional love may well determine the ultimate happiness of your marriage. Remember, *agape* can begin with just one person. It can start with you, no matter what your partner is doing. That is the genius of this love.

By giving your mate acceptance through *agape*, you will find it immeasurably easier to work out whatever problems you have. But acceptance must be given in the framework of permanent commitment. To feel that you are accepted today but just might be rejected tomorrow is of little value. The total commitment of *agape* becomes the bedrock foundation of your marriage. As you express *agape* habitually, you will have a new serenity of heart because now you are not reacting like a rubber ball to everything that happens. You are behaving consistently with a giving love that flows right from the heart of God into your heart and on to bless the life of your marriage partner.

Here is how to make *agape* the central force of your marriage:

1) Choose with your will to love your mate unconditionally and permanently through attitude, word, and action.

When God created us, He gave us a wonderful faculty in addition to minds that think and emotions that feel. He gave us a free will. With our will we want and choose, and our will becomes the most influential part of our personality. When our will exercises its power of choice, it acts for our total person and the rest of our being falls into line with what we have chosen.

Thus, we choose to apply God's scriptural principles concerning love, and we choose to give this love to our mate without limits or conditions.

2) Develop the knowledge you need in order to do the very best for the object of your love.

Knowledge is indispensable in the exercise of *agape* love. If the loving actions of *agape* are not guided by precise knowledge of your partner, they will miss the mark.

Two kinds of knowledge are involved. The first is biblical. When I became a Christian and discovered that I could and must love my wife with *agape*, I had to study the Scriptures to learn how a husband is to love his wife and what a wife needs from her husband. As our Creator, God knows how we can best relate to each other, and He has not hidden these facts from us.

Through simple Bible study a man finds that the best thing he can do for his wife is to become the kind of husband described in Ephesians 5. A woman learns that the best thing she can do for her husband is to become the kind of wife described in 1 Peter 3. A number of good books have been written on the husband/wife roles in Scripture, and you will want to read some of them as you make your own study. In brief, the husband will find as he studies the New Testament and the Song of Solomon that God has designed him to be a protective, competent leader who will take care of his wife, and a tender, kind, and courteous lover who initiates love for her. This is what his wife needs from him. The wife who studies these Scriptures will find that God has designed her to be a responder to her husband's love; one prepared to help, who can gracefully adapt to her husband's calling in life; who possesses the beauty of a gentle, quiet spirit as she respects and affirms her husband; and who continues to delight him all through his life. This is what he needs from her.

This basic design, established by God in His loving wisdom, reflects the inmost natures of husband and wife and cannot be altered by those who would try. It lies deep within the plan of God, dating from the dawn of Creation, and no matter what cultural changes people attempt to bring about in the name of unisex, the fact remains that God created us male and female with distinctive privileges and responsibilities. Men and women are *different*, thank God, and so we can enrich each other and bring the full measure of joy into our marriage.

To love your mate meaningfully, you must add personal knowledge to biblical knowledge. This must be an intelligent, intimate, perceptive knowledge of the unique individual you are married to. If you do not understand your mate's highly specialized needs and desires, you will be unable to meet them with *agape* love.

Husband, you are told in 1 Peter 3 to dwell with your wife according to knowledge. You are to be totally relaxed and at home with her because you understand her so well. Because you understand her, you will know what she desires and needs; how to meet her needs; what will make her *feel* loved; and how to do the very best for her on a consistent basis.

The wife should study her husband in the same way to discover what makes him feel loved and to find out what he desires and needs and how she can best meet those needs. This is the creative project of a lifetime for both partners. Remember that *agape* is always an appropriate love, not given to suit your own hangups, but to ensure and enhance your partner's well-being. One of the thrills of marriage is knowing that you are providing what your beloved desires!

Strangely enough, one can be loved and accepted unconditionally and still not *feel* genuinely loved. What feels like love will vary with the individual—this is why you must know your mate so well. One person may measure love by the way his material needs are met, or by tangible items such as expensive gifts. Another may feel loved when her husband helps her with the dishes. One will measure love by the amount of time spent together, or by the quality of openness and sharing of thoughts between the two. Another desperately needs to hear often the words: *I love you*. Still another measures love by physical affection—hugs and kisses. One person puts a heavy emphasis on the loyalty shown by the mate, especially in public. Another values sensitivity shown to feelings. Some will measure love by the support given to their personal growth and development. There are so many languages of love! While all I have mentioned are important, some of them will have special, even critical, significance for your mate on an emotional level. Learn what speaks love to your own partner; then express your love in ways that cannot be doubted.

If the two of you are reading this book together, set aside some time to talk about each other's feelings. Share with your mate exactly what it is that makes you *feel* loved. Always keep the discussion on a positive basis without hint of reproach for past mistakes your partner may have made. Remember, you can never enhance or rekindle the emotions of love by heaping a sense of failure on your partner. I cannot overemphasize this. *Never* in the slightest way put a feeling of guilt upon your mate.

If you are more concerned about building love in your marriage than your partner is, and you are unable to discuss your feelings together, then begin to concentrate on a deeper understanding of your mate so that you, to begin with, can learn his or her special language of love by observation and discernment.

3) Apply everything that you know in giving agape love. Pour your life into it.

Never forget that *agape* is action, not just attitude. Make a specific effort to *do* loving things for your partner daily in addition to what you *are*. The wise husband or wife listens with the heart to consider and understand what the partner needs and desires, then acts to meet those longings.

Here is how one wife met her husband's deepest needs through the knowledgeable expression of *agape:*

"This began as a bleak time for us," Sue explained. "Because of my husband's change of job we left our pleasant life in a small town and moved to the big city where nothing seemed right. The house we rented was like a prison to me. I felt as if I had lost contact with the outside world! The neighborhood was unsafe, and I had no women friends, not even one good neighbor. Our church was so far away—clear across the city. Rob worked the evening shift so I was all alone with plenty of time to feel sorry for myself. I turned to the Bible during those long, lonely evenings.

"Rob and I had been Christians for years, but we had never enjoyed the oneness in the Lord that I had hoped for. Now, as I turned to Bible study and prayer—struggling with my fears and unmet needs—the Lord directed my attention to Rob and *his* unhappiness and *his* needs. I love my husband, and I could not bear to have him living such a joyless, sterile life.

"I began asking the Lord to teach me the right way to love my husband. I searched the Scriptures to find out how to meet Rob's needs. Do you know, the Lord took me to 1 Peter 3 and kept me there for months! I used to think of verse 1 as speaking of the lost husband: 'In the same way, you wives, be submissive to your own husbands so that even if any of them are disobedient to the Word, they may be won without a word by the behavior of their wives.' Now I realized that saved husbands are not always obedient to the Word either. Many of them don't know what it says. My husband was in that category, and he needed to be 'won without a word.' *Without a word* was something new for me! I had always tried to push my husband along in the Christian life. Now I made the *choice* to love Rob by obeying 1 Peter 3:1–6 in daily behavior and attitudes. Those were conditions that had to be met if I was to obtain this promise.

"I also determined to turn all my thoughts and my heart to God and to my husband. Every day I claimed Philippians 1:6, for I knew that a good work was begun in Rob long ago. I was confident that the Lord would complete it—now that I wasn't standing in His way. I also read Psalm 112 daily as an affirmation of God's purpose for Rob, putting his name in there. What a beautiful portrait of the righteous man. This is what Rob is becoming.

"It's been six months now, and I can tell you there is a transformation going on here that Rob and I can hardly believe. God's Word is absolutely true if we just do what it says in faith! We are developing such a beautiful relationship with each other, with God at the center of our marriage. Rob and I have a wonderful time together now. It is as grand as I always believed it could be. Fifty years old, and I am so in love with my husband! Such a beautiful life! Rob now wants to do things for me and with me. He seems to really enjoy talking with me, reading Scripture to me, and sharing insights about spiritual matters. Now the Lord has miraculously answered Rob's prayer that he would be able to work days and be home with me in the evenings.

"Rob told me recently that for a long time he had had one great desire—that the joy of his salvation would be restored. And now, Rob says, that desire has been fulfilled! The Lord allowed me to have a part in giving my husband what he wanted most when I chose to love him with *agape* love."

This wife has given us a concrete example of the way *agape* can transform the love-life of marriage when even one partner chooses to do the very best for her beloved—-the best, scripturally, and the best, personally. (The two always seem to go together.) *Agape* love often clashes head-on with our old learned habits of conditional loving, so when you choose the *agape* way as Sue did, you have an adventure before you.

I must caution you on one important point. Please don't start loving with *agape* just because you want to reform your mate. This is not *agape* at all, but another form of conditional love. Change comes only from inner motivation. So accept your partner exactly the way he or she is now and seek to change your own behavior in accord with biblical standards to lovingly meet your mate's needs. The rest is accomplished by the Holy Spirit working through the Word of God.

You may be interested to know that almost all of the individuals mentioned at the beginning of this chapter did set their feet on the *agape* way. Faced with "no response" in their marriage, they had only two options: give up or learn to love a new way. Quentin quickly became discouraged and gave up. Tragic disintegration of home and family resulted. Una, on the other hand, has already seen her marriage totally transformed. The others are faithfully continuing to love their mates with *agape*, some with dramatic personal results. Barbara, for instance, has become a radiant Christian in the process, and the change in Eric has been remarkable. He is a new man in Christ.

As a counselor for many years I can promise this: no one who has ever really tried the *agape* way has regretted it. After all, it is commanded by God, and He always has surprises of love for those who obey Him!

11

The Secret of Staying in Love (Especially for Newlyweds)

It is a remarkable fact that while millions of men and women have no difficulty in falling in love, at least half of that number seem unable to *stay* in love. This chapter offers the secret of staying in love for any couple interested in a lifelong love affair. The secret in one potent word is: *intimacy*.

Although couples of all ages and at all stages of marriage can use this information to improve their relationships, we want to speak directly to couples just beginning their married life. Ideally, this is where the intimacy building process should begin.

As a family physician and premarriage counselor, I have had some part in preparing hundreds of couples for the adventure of marriage. It is interesting to observe the varying attitudes of these couples as they approach the most significant event of their lives.

Some come into my office wrapped in a romantic haze that can scarcely be penetrated. They are walking on clouds, feeding on dreams, and feeling no need for counsel or advice. "Happily ever after" seems guaranteed from their point of view. It is impossible for them to believe that their emotional euphoria could ever be eroded by daily routine, growing irritations, competing attractions, or financial and family pressures. After all, they are in love, and isn't that all that matters?

Some come in rather anxiously, afraid of admitting any inadequacy within themselves or any need for information. They think that whatever happiness they feel now is going to be so much better after marriage. It is as if they are counting on the *fact* of marriage to provide them with something it can never deliver. In reality, marriage will magnify whatever problems they are trying to overlook in their present relationship or in themselves. (To paraphrase John F. Kennedy, we should not ask what our marriage can do for us, but what we can do for our marriage.)

Others are in a hurry to take care of the premarriage business as one more in a long list of errands, carelessly confident that their marriage can succeed without any instruction in love. A few tips on sex and a blood test to meet state requirements will suffice! Their high expectations invariably are based on their partner's ability to meet all of their wants, needs, wishes, and desires for the next fifty years. Thus their happiness is going to depend on how well their partner performs for them—always a shaky business.

Sadly, I see many of these couples later under very different circumstances. Now, buried under a load of problems, they welcome every word that can help them work their way out of marital conflict and grief.

Then there are the couples I consider fortunate—those with realistic goals; eager to learn everything they can about developing a positive, loving relationship that will endure; and ready to put conscious, intelligent effort and careful planning into the development of the intimacy that can keep them in love for a lifetime.

Van and Terri, for instance, drove eight hundred miles for premarriage counseling. They came well prepared, having already listened to our counseling tapes and having studied our book, *Intended for Pleasure*, as well as other Christian materials on marriage. They had written their questions out in advance, anticipating problems that could arise and planning how to prevent them. It was obvious that they expected a wonderful life and did not want to miss out on any good thing that would enhance their marriage. Van and Terri believed their relationship was worth all the planning and effort they could possibly put into it.

They were totally committed to the challenge of staying in love for a lifetime and enjoying every minute of it!

So together we discussed the principles of building intimacy in marriage—the principles that every newlywed couple should be putting into practice. The urgency of this can be understood by noting that the median duration of marriage before divorce is only seven years and, according to researchers, a mere three to five years for people drawn together by sexual attraction. *Now is the time for intimacy!* should be engraved in every newlywed's home—or heart.

What is intimacy? It is a fashionable word these days that describes the kind of relationship people have always longed for. Intimacy (derived from the Latin *intimus,* meaning inmost) refers to the state of being most private, most personal in relationship. It depicts a special quality of emotional closeness between two people in which both are constantly alert and responsive to fluctuations of feeling and to the well-being of the other. It can mean to understand and to be fully understood by one who cares for us deeply.

Of course, to become so finely tuned to each other demands time and conscious effort from both partners, but the resulting closeness lifts the relationship out of the commonplace and into the unique and irreplaceable.

Dr. Helen Kaplan terms intimacy "an important ingredient in the quality of love and of life. A high degree of intimacy between two lovers or spouses contributes to the happiness and emotional stability of both. All activities are more enjoyable and life is richer and more colorful when shared with an intimate partner.

"An intimate relationship acts as a buffer, providing shelter from the pressures and tensions of daily life," Dr. Kaplan observes, warning that "without intimate relationships we tend to get lonely and become depressed. The availability of intimate relationships is an important determinant of how well we master life's crises."[1]

There is no intimacy as precious or rewarding as that which can be experienced in marriage. When it is absent the effects range from dull to dismal to devastating. As Dr. William S. Appleton has pointed out, "It is essential to remember that marital dullness is *not* confined to middle and later years; indeed it can and does occur in the first year of marriage."

He calls boredom the warning signal with "preventive maintenance . . . the answer." And he emphasizes that "people are now less willing to tolerate boredom. . . . Magazines and television have raised expectations. Americans expect the good life materially and interpersonally. They want fulfilling marriages, high-quality leisure time, exciting sex, warm intimacy, stimulating conversation, good-looking bright spouses 24 hours a day! Unfortunately, their knowledge of and patience with necessary marital maintenance is often so minimal that their chances of achieving their high relationship goals are almost zero."[2]

Certainly, an emotionally flat, chronically dull marriage signals the need for positive steps toward building intimacy, injecting new life into the relationship. Recently a young husband said to me with a note of despair, "My wife and I have already lost touch with each other." It was a graphic description of their lack of intimacy, for to experience intimacy is to *touch*— emotionally, physically, mentally, and spiritually.

Here are some of the strands that make up the bond of intimacy between a husband and wife. They are given in no particular order, and you may have others of your own to add.

- Physical touching of an affectionate, non-sexual nature
- Shared feelings
- Closeness without inhibitions
- Absence of psychological defenses
- Open communication and honesty
- Intellectual agreement on major issues
- Spiritual harmony
- Sensitive appreciation of the mate's physical and emotional responses
- Similar values held
- Imparted secrets
- Genuine understanding

- Mutual confidence
- A sense of warmth, safety, and relaxation when together
- Sensuous nearness
- Sexual pleasures lovingly shared
- Signs of love freely given and received
- Mutual responsibility and caring
- Abiding trust

Couples who enjoy intimacy have their own special tokens of it. One wife, speaking of the ease of long intimacy, defined it as "understanding without words . . . family jokes that don't have to be explained . . . and a warm back in a wide bed."

In general, intimacy consists of a blending of the five facets of love that have been described in previous chapters. It does not happen easily in a marriage for there are too many hindrances that would impede its growth. And it will never happen automatically. To use W. H. Auden's description, an intimate longterm marriage "is not the involuntary result of fleeting emotion but *the creation of time and will.*" *Time* and *will* are primary factors in developing the intimacy that will cause you to stay in love! Auden concludes that this makes a marriage "infinitely more interesting and significant than any romance." As newlyweds set out, determined to build intimacy because it is worth doing and because it offers them lifetime rewards, they will find Auden's conclusion to be true. Their marriage will become the most interesting, significant relationship on this earth in their view. Romantic fiction will pale in comparison with the realities they enjoy every day.

But *time* and *will* must be joined by the *knowledge* and *patience* Dr. Appleton referred to—"knowledge f and patience with necessary marital maintenance." If marriages are made in heaven, their maintenance occurs in an earthly setting, which requires not only knowledge but also patience in the process.

Biblically, the Lord allotted one year of concentrated togetherness for newlyweds in order to establish the patterns of intimacy that would last a lifetime. "When a man hath taken a new wife, he shall not go out to war, neither shall he be charged with any business: but he shall be free at home one year, and shall cheer up his wife which he hath taken" (Deuteronomy 24:5).

The Hebrew word translated "to cheer up" meant: to delight his wife, to know her, and to discover what would be pleasing to her.

In today's economy very few men can afford to take off for a year of honeymooning, but important scriptural principles are here for every newly married couple to consider:

(1) Nothing is as important as the health of your marriage and your growth in oneness.

(2) To concentrate on knowing each other and building an intimate relationship is pleasing to the Lord.

(3) It takes time spent *together* to properly lay the foundations of marriage.

(4) It is essential that the husband learn how to meet his wife's needs.

(5) Knowledge of one's mate is necessary in order to live according to biblical patterns. You must know your partner in depth if you are to love, understand, help, and encourage.

(6) Marriage mates are meant to be teammates yoked together to serve God effectively. Becoming teammates takes time and cooperation in an atmosphere as free from distraction as possible.

(7) According to the Creator's wisdom, the first year is crucial in any marriage and should be lived with care and forethought.

Another principle may be observed. It is that strong marriages are in a nation's best interests. So much of the health of society depends on the marriage unit, that in Israel the forming of a strong marriage took priority over business or military duties. Evidently the nation's *internal* strength was considered of primary importance.

Here are specific ways to build intimacy in your marriage along with some hindrances to avoid. Because we experience intimacy by touching in the different areas of our relationship, these principles will come under four headings: Touching—Physically; Touching—Emotionally; Touching—Mentally; and Touching—Spiritually

1) Touching—Physically

I am referring to non-sexual physical caresses between husband and wife—of cuddling, snuggling, hugging, holding hands, sitting and sleeping close to each other, not as an occasional happening, but as an integral part of your daily life.

Touching is the most natural act in the world, and our need for it is more basic than our need for sex. Sex falls into the category of *desire*, for unmarried people can live happy, fulfilled lives without it. But the caring touch of another human being is a *need* that should not be ignored. At birth, touch was our first line of communication. The cuddling and loving we received was necessary for our emotional development, even for our physical well-being. Now that we are adults, very little has changed. We still have a deep need for the warmth, reassurance, and intimacy of nonsexual touching whether we are conscious of it or not. Often we turn to sex when what we really want is the comfort of loving closeness. As one husband observed, "Sex is a lot of extra effort when all you need is a real warm hug!" Psychologists believe that American preoccupation with sex these days is really a longing for the emotionally supportive physical affection that every human craves, but which has been in short supply in our culture.

If you are in doubt about how to begin developing intimacy physically, consider Webster's definition of *caress:* "An act of endearment; a tender or loving embrace, touch. To touch, stroke, pat; tenderly, lovingly, or softly." Begin doing these things, weaving simple physical touch into the fabric of your daily life. For instance, hold hands at the table when you pray. Take some time for closeness early in the morning and snuggle together at night. Sit on the couch so that you are touching in some way, rather than choosing chairs across the room. Hug and kiss when you go your separate ways for the day and do the same when you come together in the evening.

As you do this habitually you will share the same good sensations of warmth, security, and psychological satisfaction that you felt in childhood when you were held close by your mother. This

136

is the tangible base of your intimate relationship. It is real because you can touch it.

Betty Ford in *The Times of My Life* says, "What stands out most in my memory about Mamie and Ike (Eisenhower) is their affection for each other. . . . I document my observation with photographs. So many pictures of them look unposed, as if they'd been caught in the act of touching." She recalls what Mamie, then widowed and eighty years old, said about her husband's "wonderful hands." "Every knuckle," she said, "was broken from football or whatever, but I always felt in all the years we were married that I could grab onto them when I felt sick or worried, and nothing was ever going to happen to me."

A young wife expressed her need for tangible expressions of caring in this poem to her husband:

Please—
Come take my hand
  Let's walk!!

Give me you—
  Eyes saying—Hi!
  Glances saying—I care!
  Handholds that let me know you were only teasing;
  Hugs saying—Thank you for being you!
  Kisses that—gently want me;

Then Love—
  That says, I'll be here tomorrow
  and everyday hereafter.[3]

Physical contact is absolutely essential in building the thrill of intimacy and kindling the flame of romantic love between husband and wife. I have observed that the people who come to my office saying, "I love my partner but I'm just not *in love* with him (or her)," are the ones who are having little affectionate touching in their marriage—no hugs or love pats, few kisses, no snuggling at night.

While physical touching is the easiest and most effective way to begin to build intimacy in your marriage, several hindrances sometimes exist and can become problems if allowed to continue.

First, many young couples who built an intense love relationship by caressing while dating often quit affectionate touching after marriage. The reason? Now they are using touch only as a sexual signal to communicate a readiness to make love. At other times they carefully stay apart lest an affectionate gesture be misinterpreted.

Couples must break the habit of using touch exclusively as a signal for sex. This will deprive you of the warmth and physical tenderness that every marriage should have. It may be interesting to know that building true intimacy in marriage will decrease your need for sexual signals. A greater openness will exist between you, a more comfortable relationship even in the sensitive area of sex. Many times the wife feels more free to initiate sex. Husband and wife are relaxed with each other and yet beautifully sensitive to the feelings and desires of the other. So I encourage you to keep up the physical closeness that helped you to fall in love in the first place. And rid yourself of the myth that touching itself must always lead to sex. Lovingly talk it over so that you both agree that touching casually and often will signal your growing intimacy. You must be able to touch each other in a relaxed way without fear of rebuff or misunderstanding.

The second hindrance is caused by the individual who goes into marriage convinced that he or she is just not naturally affectionate. Some are quick to tell me that they are different from other people . . . that they do not like to be touched . . . that it is not their nature. In most cases this can be traced to their early upbringing. But whatever the reason, anyone can *learn* to express his love through physical closeness. Anyone can *become* affectionate, even in a few months, with the right motivation and encouragement. Remember that the Christian does not have to see himself in a certain mold: "This is just the way I am, so I can't change." It is a fact of the Christian life that we do not have to remain as we are, because God will change us as we are obedient to Him. We have the spiritual resources to make any changes that are needed.

Couples who have experienced this change say that their new patterns of affectionate touching are bringing them feelings of comfort, support, and optimism that are wonderful. They have found out that giving and receiving physical affection adds a new dimension of pleasure to their life together.

But what if you have developed some negative attitudes toward each other? Does that mean you have to stay apart until you are over your anger? The answer is no! Therapists have found that actions do change attitudes and that physical closeness should be resumed immediately. Even when couples have experienced years of hostility and bickering, they are helped by learning to touch warmly and intimately.

One husband told me that his wife was not an affectionate person. When he began to practice the principles of building intimacy, it took months of patient, consistent, gentle, loving advances before she began to respond. But recently she said to him (as they cuddled in bed on a Saturday morning), "This is so much fun. I wonder why we waited so long to do it!"

2) Touching—Emotionally

A university professor who has taught a class on love for twelve years says that the most common problem discussed in his class is the basic difficulty people have in forming a deep, meaningful relationship with another person. Obviously, touching emotionally is far more complicated than touching physically! When we consider the complexities of emotional intimacy we can understand why the Lord set aside the first year for newlyweds to concentrate solely on each other. Creating emotional intimacy involves the meeting and merging of two different sets of emotions. The challenges are compounded because the two personalities learning to harmonize are masculine and feminine.

"A man who can understand his own wife can understand just about anything," a homespun philosopher mused, and, indeed, Scripture seems to indicate that women are more delicate and far more emotionally complicated than men. The godly wife also is incredibly valuable, according to Proverbs 31. Her value goes beyond the most priceless jewel. But she must be intimately known and understood to be appreciated. Thus, Peter, in his first epistle, counsels husbands to give top priority to understanding their wives: "Ye husbands, dwell with them according to knowledge, giving honor unto the wife. . . . Be ye all of one mind. . . ." Husbands should study their wives so that they can feel at home with them, totally at ease together, with full knowledge of each other. Craig Massey suggests that a man must learn to understand his wife's responses to herself, to him, and to the world's influence on her.

But if the greater responsibility has been put on the man, it still takes the wholehearted cooperation of both partners to develop the emotional intimacy that will keep them in love.

Emotional intimacy begins when two people deliberately share the same world—sharing time, interests, feelings, thoughts, goals, and ideals. It is possible for "in love" newlyweds to quickly develop two different worlds like separate continents without bridges *unless* they make a concerted and consistent effort to spend their free time together, developing absorbing interests in common, and doing the tasks of life in partnership, side by side. That most prized relationship of understanding and being fully understood by one who deeply cares comes into being as both are willing to communicate with each other—sharing experiences, dreams, fears, and secrets they would tell to no one else. Talking in private about private matters builds emotional intimacy as nothing else can! Many students of love believe that sharing is the key, that it is growing separateness in the minds of marriage partners that kills love. Couples, then, must knit their individual lives together in that important first year to form one pattern of intimacy, consisting of many threads of togetherness.

Intimacy can grow only in a place of safety. When husband and wife are afraid of hurt, rebuff, criticism, and misunderstanding, they will find it difficult to touch and share freely. So if you want real intimacy in your marriage, you will have to establish trust in your relationship.

God's Word shows how to do this in two concise statements:

"Love covers over a multitude of sins" (1 Peter 4:8 NIV); and "Love builds up" (1 Corinthians 8:1 NIV). In other words you must: (1) overlook mistakes and never criticize; and (2) always encourage and give your partner the gift of sympathetic understanding.

As a counselor I observe many people attempting to improve their marriage partners by criticizing them, pointing out their faults and mistakes. But this never changes anyone for the better. It only puts miles of emotional distance between a husband and wife who may be secretly longing for closeness.

The truth about criticism is almost startling when fully grasped: criticism can actually be the death blow to love, intimacy, and all the good things you want to build in your marriage. So think before you speak! Remember the potent power of praise and form the habit of consistently building up rather than tearing down. I do not recall when my wife and I last criticized each other. After years of edifying, we are not even conscious of personal flaws in the other because we are so caught up in the pleasure of living every day together. Gaye and I can enthusiastically recommend this pattern of interaction to couples just beginning their marriage because we know that it works so well.

There is another element that will contribute to your mutual trust. In plain words, the rule should be: never let your partner down in something that really matters to him or her. The application of this rule will be determined by your partner—not you. You might feel that you are behaving correctly, yet this may clash violently with your partner's emotional perceptions of what he or she needs from you. A marriage often begins with fantasies and unreasonable expectations of a partner who will be all things, perfectly meeting every desire. But wise newlyweds will learn to replace these dreams (which could never be fulfilled by an imperfect human being) with realistic expectations. This requires a dialogue of loving honesty. What can you realistically expect from each other? What really matters to you down in the fibers of your unique emotional makeup?

One couple, the Xaviers, gave me examples from their own

marriage. *She* said, "My husband thought I was being too demanding when I asked him to give up his plans so he could go with me to the dentist—an emergency trip. Until he understood that I was simply terrified of the prospect and I *needed* his support. If he had refused I would have felt he had failed me badly. But because we discussed it, he understood my need and met it in a loving way." *He* said, "I will never forget the sight of my wife dropping everything else to type my research paper—and staying up half the night to do it. She really bailed me out without a word of complaint because I explained how important it was to me."

The kind of dialogue that leads to genuine understanding is far more than conversation. It involves *listening to each other from the very beginning of the conversation* with an attentive ear to what the other person really is saying and feeling. Communication has been defined as the ability to send and receive messages accurately—not only factual messages, but signals of an emotional nature. To learn to listen and to communicate is an essential part of perfecting the art of loving.

John Powell calls dialogue "an act of purest love." He explains, "The listening and speaking of dialogue are each directed to the other. Dialogue is essentially other-centered. . . .

"There are no winners and losers in dialogue," he points out, "only winners. Neither partner is ever required to give up or give in but only to give, to give of himself. In a dialogue we can never end up with less than we were but only more. To live in dialogue with another is to live twice. Joys are doubled by exchange and burdens are cut in half by sharing."[4]

These three guidelines should be followed as you practice communication in the early days of your marriage:

(1) Talk more freely about your feelings, but not in such a way that your partner feels rebuked or criticized.

(2) Be willing to show your vulnerable side to your mate. A cardinal rule of developing intimacy is: Dare to be needy; do not be afraid to *say*, "I need you."

(3) Remember that silence is almost always a negative feedback unless it is accompanied by nonverbal signals that your

partner shares your feelings, such as by a squeeze of the hand or a smile.

Obviously, to build intimacy and establish trust, any emotional conflict must be settled quickly. In fact, I give this guideline in premarriage counseling: *Never go to bed with unresolved conflict*. The biblical principles are: "Let not the sun go down upon your wrath" (Ephesians 4:26) and "Forgive . . . as Christ forgave" (Colossians 3:13). Conflicts are inevitable in any marriage, but they become problems only when they are not quickly and lovingly resolved. Real love acts as the inhibitant to anger. When you love someone and have developed a satisfying level of intimacy, anger disappears rapidly. It is a relief to forgive and forget and to feel close to each other again. You will both need to recognize times when your behavior is less loving than it should be, and readily admit this to your partner with a sincere "I'm sorry." An apology is recognition of the fact that your relationship is so important to you that you want to keep it in good repair. When you "keep up" with each other through emotional intimacy, the relationship can be easily restored. Keeping up is far easier than "catching up" after years of emotional distance.

Some of the hindrances that can pose serious threats to your emotional intimacy show up like warning lights in this letter from Walt, a heartbroken husband:

> My wife's divorce proceedings are just days away. By way of my attorney, I postponed answering the papers, but have run out of time.
> There is no doubt, Dr. Wheat, that I am guilty of most everything you warned against. Neither Yvonne nor I were fully aware of our obligation to God and each other when we made our vows. As time went on we managed to draw away from each other by not sharing in each other's world. Yvonne placed manipulative conditions on our sex life. I had to do certain things such as wash dishes, etc., to win a few intimate moments. I realize that I failed to follow most of the guidelines you give for love. It was not a matter of not loving her in my heart, but my blindness to her needs, as well as my own selfishness. My job requires quite a bit

of time, which was bad enough, but I also didn't open the rest of my life to her as I should.

Her parents never let us be, constantly interfering with our lives. Her mother constantly wanted her to "come by" and go places with her. So I did not really feel necessary in her life. I began to come home to supper on the stove and a quickly scribbled note about "gone so and so with Mama."

In my failure I didn't set about to improve our situation. Instead, I found ways to amuse myself, and in time our lives became two different paths, and our home a pit stop for sleep. Our separate paths began to bring about sexual hunger in me, and once again I failed. I had an affair to try to counter this frustration. I knew this was sin and my conscience ate at me. I see now that I was substituting selfishness for the patience I should have had and thinking only how to fulfill myself.

When I finally came to the point of suggesting that we seek help for our marriage, it was too late for Yvonne. I have tried fervently to seek forgiveness and to reconcile, but her response has been hatred. . . . Our four-year-old prays each time I am with her for God to help Mommy and Daddy get back together. . . .

As Walt's letter illustrates, in-laws can be a most serious hindrance to establishing intimacy. The Lord recognized this in His commands to Adam (before sin had entered into the human race). He gave Adam two commands and one of them was to keep in-laws out of marriage. Looking down the corridors of time at future causes of marital disharmony, God said that in-laws should not be involved in your marriage—that an entirely new social unit is to be established. This means that separation from both sets of parents is a necessity:

Physically. Do not live with your parents after marriage. Do not even spend a great deal of time together. I occasionally hear of couples who take their in-laws with them on the honeymoon trip. No matter how well-intentioned this is, it sets up an undesirable pattern. Intimacy in marriage is a private thing. It is something you just do not share with others. You might have a good time with a group of people on a trip, but that is not intimacy. Real intimacy can flower only when you are alone together. By the way, never discuss intimate marital problems with your parents.

Emotionally. Do not marry if you cannot be emotionally independent of your own family. Recent research indicates that "going home to mama" when conflicts appear is as prevalent in marriage today as ever in spite of the new thirst for independence. Do not allow a parent to fill an emotional role that should be reserved for your mate alone. No genuinely loving parent will expect this or seek it.

Financially. Do not marry if you cannot maintain a household. Help in financing education should be accepted only if you can be completely free from domination by those providing the funds.

Another hindrance to intimacy expressed so vividly in Walt's letter was that of living in separate worlds until coming home for both meant only taking a pit stop for sleep!

This lonely state of affairs begins when a young couple does not make any effort to build a new life together. Instead they each pursue their separate interests and sometimes keep their separate friends. In a *Moody Monthly* article, "Satan's Doctrines of Marriage," Craig Massey points out that Satan's lie says: *"You can spend time away from one another without hurting the marriage relationship."* No wonder this is a favorite satanic lie! Intimacy—physical, emotional, mental, and spiritual—simply cannot be accomplished by separation, and it is this intimacy that fulfills and satisfies, which causes two to become one according to God's design.

The third serious hindrance to emotional intimacy is that ubiquitous annoyance we call the television set. Some TV shows are informative and enjoyable, of course. But few people seem to have the discipline required to choose only the best programs and keep the set turned off otherwise. In premarriage counseling I encourage every couple to refrain from getting a TV set for the first year. I tell them that television robs them of wonderful hours that could be spent together, sharing and learning to relate to each other. There can be no giving, no receiving, when you have your eyes and mind glued to the set.

Dennis Guernsey in *Thoroughly Married* says:

> It's folly to try to communicate with the television blaring in the background, in between football timeouts. . . . Quality time requires a focus of attention that is impossible to achieve if the slightest distraction persists. Most of us would be shocked if we totaled up the amount of face-to-face time we spent with each other during the last week, the last month, or the last year. Weeks can go by without a meaningful time for the sharing of our lives.

He calls attention to the special value in deliberately and regularly setting aside time to be with each other:

> Many couples successfully manage the "hurt" in their relationship because they know for sure there will be a time and an opportunity to work their problems through. In contrast, the smallest annoyance in a marriage can become unbearable if it appears it will be there forever. . . . We end up trying to go in all directions at once and then wonder why we've lost touch with each other.

No husband or wife should take the matter of emotional intimacy lightly. Intimacy will cause you to stay in love. But without intimacy one or both of you may be strongly tempted to seek it elsewhere. Dr. Mary Ann Bartusis in a study of marital triangles found that all too often an affair occurs with the spouse's best friend. Why? Because human beings have an "insatiable quest" for a meaningful one-to-one relationship that is not being satisfied within the marriage; and because so many opportunities for intimacy exist with the marriage partner's "best friend." Intimate talks are often a key factor in developing the feeling of being in love. Dr. Bartusis suggests that familiarity, availability, and acceptance are the keys—conditions easily fulfilled with a close friend of the family.[5]

So, invest in emotional intimacy with your own partner and find a happiness that carries with it no regrets or bitter aftereffects

3) Touching—Mentally

This level of intimacy involves coming to an agreement about all the important issues that determine the direction of your life It requires practice in making intelligent plans for your lifestyle and the well-being of your family. Couples who learn to develop this kind of intimacy find real pleasure in setting goals together and then accomplishing them together.

One example will suffice. The area of financial habits is crucial to the future of the marriage. Experts believe that 50 percent of all divorces are now caused by financial disagreements, and with the growing instability of our economy, this number is sure to rise. Just the frustrations of keeping a home and family solvent these days are enough to create conflicts unless the financial difficulties become challenges that draw husband and wife together. A beautiful intimacy can develop as husband and wife face and overcome the budget shortages together. It is not just a matter of eliminating causes for conflict, but the positive value of working together to build a God-honoring life of financial freedom that makes this such an important aspect of intimacy-building.

George and Marjean Fooshee in *You Can Beat the Money Squeeze* warn of "the debt trap." They define a trap as attractive, easy to get into, and almost impossible to escape from—an accurate description of the credit card lifestyle. The easy credit available for so long in our culture has taught people to overspend consistently, hoping to make enough in the future to pay for what they are using up today. Probably the majority of married couples today find themselves more or less financially entrapped.

Newlyweds who want to establish a pattern of financial freedom should be very sensitive to these warning signs:

- You are preoccupied with thoughts about money, at the expense of thoughts about God.
- You don't give what you feel God wants you to give.
- You are not at peace to live on what God has provided.
- You argue within your family about money matters.
- You can't or don't pay credit cards debts in full each month.
- You need or have considered a consolidation loan.
- You receive notices of past-due accounts.
- You charge items because you can't pay cash.
- You use spending as emotional therapy.

- You spend impulsively.
- You invade savings to meet current expenses.
- Your net worth does not increase annually.
- You "just can't save."
- You are underinsured.
- You wish you had a plan for spending and saving and are frustrated because you don't.

The goal to be financially free requires two basic decisions, the Fooshees say: (1) Decide at the outset that you will not spend what you do not have. (2) Trust God instead of trusting a loan.

Christian Financial Concepts, a non-profit organization headed by Larry Burkett, can give you knowledgeable and practical help in carrying out these decisions by handling your finances according to biblical principles and wise economic policies. I highly recommend their books, counseling cassette albums, and their seminars that are held in churches across the country. Write to the organization at 209-A Norcross-Tucker Road, Norcross, GA 30071 for further details.

Finances always prove to be divisive in marriage no matter what your economic level unless the two of you develop the right attitudes together—another important step in intimacy growth.

4) Touching—Spiritually

Another of my premarriage recommendations is: *Have some Bible study together every day.* This is the basic way to develop spiritual intimacy. As the Word of God courses through your minds, you are shaped and transformed together into new people with united attitudes and goals and with a common outlook that comes from taking in God's viewpoint of every aspect of life. It is really the responsibility of the husband to initiate daily Bible study. If you don't know how, one way is to listen together to Bible teaching on cassette. Bible Believers Cassettes, Inc., a *free-loan* library, offers the best in Bible teaching by the finest teachers in the English-speaking world today. There are more than ten thousand different messages available with many on the subject of marriage and the Christian home. You may wish to begin with these. Send one dollar for your catalog to Bible Believers Cassettes, Inc., 130 N. Spring St., Springdale, AR 72764.

I also recommend that every newly married couple become actively involved in a local church where they can learn and grow and serve the Lord in company with other people who will get to know them well and to care for their well-being.

Nothing can draw a couple closer than genuine, heart-searching prayer together. I appreciate the testimony my wife Gaye shared in *Intended for Pleasure* concerning the rewards of spiritual intimacy. She wrote,

> Now that we are Christians, I know that the love Ed has for me is the same kind of love that Christ has for me. I am safe and secure in that love. I know that I can always talk to my husband and that I can trust his wisdom as the spiritual leader of our family. As we have become so used to pouring our hearts out together in prayer, we now are free to communicate about anything to each other. We are not afraid to expose ourselves and our faults, because we know that we accept each other just as we are, with all our frailties and faults and good points. How wonderful it is to know that I am not on a performance basis: No matter how poorly I perform, I am still going to be loved. And that *has* to make me perform better.

At the beginning of this chapter I referred to Van and Terri, a couple who came eight hundred miles for premarriage counseling. It has been a pleasure to hear of their progress in building a close, intimate, and wonderfully happy marriage. They started off wisely with a private honeymoon in the mountainous beauty but inexpensive facilities of a state park. Their goal was not to go somewhere to be entertained, but to focus on each other, and they report that they had a meaningful time together that will never be forgotten.

Now they have agreed on a specific goal for their life. When Van receives his graduate degree, they will be going to Africa where he plans to teach. While he completes his education, Terri is working, but their lives are carefully integrated. He helps her with the housework, and she works with him on the preparation of his papers. In fact, she is also auditing a course he teaches, and they are experiencing a real intellectual intimacy.

Terri comes from a warm, united home, while Van's parents are individualists who lead virtually separate lives. They have already agreed to model their home after the example of Terri's parents, and to fulfill this plan, they give their relationship and their "face to face" time top priority. Because their financial resources are slim, they have a carefully planned budget and enjoy inexpensive activities—exploring every resource of their area of the country in the process. She makes most of her clothes, and he is tremendously supportive of her efforts, even going with her to choose materials. He is quick to show appreciation and lets her know how thankful he is for her willingness to prepare the dinner meal after a hard day at work.

With accurate information concerning sexual adjustment at the beginning of their marriage and with a loving openness of communication, they already have developed a satisfying sex life.

Personality clashes have been avoided through forethought and understanding. Terri had found Van's strength and forcefulness appealing, but she thought there might be difficulties because of her own stubborn and independent nature. However, Van values her ability to make decisions and to cope with challenging situations. While abdicating none of his leadership role, he is encouraging her to use her strong characteristics in the most positive way.

Terri and Van often share spiritual insights. While they are cleaning up the kitchen together, they memorize and discuss Bible verses. As committed Christians, they have an active involvement in a local church and are growing together spiritually.

A close friend says their relationship is characterized by togetherness, and by their constant concern for each other. "They are always looking for ways to help each other," the friend observes.

In this day of disintegrating marriages, I would judge their chances for a good, enduring marriage and an evergrowing love to be almost 100 percent. Their secret: intimacy!

12

A Pattern for Lovers

Every married couple with a Bible in their home should become experts on the one book of the Bible devoted exclusively to love and marriage. I refer to "The Song of Songs, which is Solomon's." The Song of Solomon gives us the pattern of married love as God intended it to be, revealed in such striking detail that it can serve as a practical model for our own marriages almost three thousand years after it was written.

Through the inspiration of the Holy Spirit, we are told of a marriage between the king of Israel and a beautiful, unsophisticated country girl whom he met in the northern vineyards of his kingdom. At this point it may sound like one of those storybook tales that end, "And they lived happily ever after." But this is no pretty fantasy spun by some story teller. It is the Word of God relating truthfully, as always, the events experienced by one couple and the words and emotions they expressed that portray for all time the love-life in marriage that honors and pleases God.

It is hardly surprising that Scripture speaks so clearly on the subject of love and sexual fulfillment in marriage. After all, the Bible deals with every other area of human behavior. And we need more than admonitions as we enter into the complicated relationship of marriage; we need examples to follow! What *is* remarkable is the range and degree of practical insights to be gleaned from the Song, applicable to any marriage in any civilization. Only the guiding hand of the Creator could have made this small book of exquisite love poetry about a king and queen in 945 B.C. (or thereabouts) so amazingly relevant to the average couple today. Again we see proof that God's principles concerning marriage transcend time and cultural differences and will always work when applied. In just eight short chapters constituting the world's greatest romantic literature, the Song of Solomon not only shows today's husband and wife *how* to love each other, but realistically presents problems of marriage and the principles for solving them.

As you and your partner study this wonderful little book, you will discover how to obey God in your marriage by being very much in love and very expressive of that love while working out your natural differences.

Of course, it is impossible to make a thorough study of the Song of Solomon in one chapter, and we will not try. Instead, we want to help you enhance your love-life by emphasizing principles and conclusions drawn by the finest Bible scholars of recent times. I trust this will whet your appetite for more study on your own.

"Which way do you interpret the Song of Solomon?" a young Christian (a student) asked me recently. "I've heard that some people say it's talking about marriage and some say it's talking about spiritual things—Jesus Christ and His love for us. Which interpretation is right?"

"Both views are correct," I explained, "in the sense that you could not have one without the other. The New Testament makes it clear that marriage is intended to be a reflection on earth of the love relationship between Christ and His church. So, whenever the Bible speaks of marriage as God designed it, we are going to find applications to the spiritual relationship we enjoy with our Lord. On the other hand, as we learn more about Jesus Christ and His love for us, we will know more about the way we should behave in marriage. The principle is, 'Husbands, love your wives, even as Christ also loved the church, and gave himself for it' (Ephesians 5:25)."

152

"You mean all that is in the Song of Solomon?" the young man asked.

"Yes," I said. "Look at the way the bridegroom in the Song loves his wife. You'll find innumerable parallels to the way the Savior loves His people—the way He loves you personally. If you study how the bride responds to the bridegroom, you can learn a lot about how you are to respond to the Savior on a spiritual level. Just remember that the primary teaching of the book concerns love and marriage. These truths should never be spiritualized away."

"Okay," he nodded. "You're saying that the Bible communicates truth on different levels at the same time. So we can learn about marriage from the Song of Solomon and also see the spiritual dimensions of the book without any contradiction."

Later, with a grin, he showed me his literature textbook which analyzed a brief poem at length, explaining its "three tiers of meaning." "The man in this poem was literally writing about sundown," he said, "but also about the decay of civilizations, and about his own death, all at the same time. If poets can do that, I guess people shouldn't be surprised that God's Word contains different applications of truth in one book."

This young Christian's questions are understandable in light of the confusion that has reigned in the past concerning the Song of Solomon. In fact, no book of the Bible has been as attacked or misunderstood through the ages as this one. It may sound strange to contemporary ears, but for centuries theologians did not want to admit the plain truth: that the Song of Solomon was speaking of godly marriage between a husband and wife who loved each other!

We need to understand that from the beginning some of Satan's strongest attacks on the biblical viewpoint have been mounted against Christian marriage. To undermine biblical truth in this area, Satan effectively used the philosophies of the pagan world to permeate the church. The attitude of the Gentile pagan in the ancient world toward love, marriage, and sex clashed head-on with the biblical view as given in Genesis 1 and 2; Proverbs 5;

153

Jesus' teachings in the Gospels and His attendance at the wedding feast; 1 Corinthians 7:1-5; 1 Timothy 4:1-5; Hebrews 13:4; Ephesians 5:22-33; *and* the Song of Solomon.

What *did* the pagan believe about sexual love in marriage? While the Bible taught that marriage was good, that human sexuality was created and commanded by God for marriage, and that marriage with its one-flesh relationship provided a sacred picture of Jesus Christ and the church, the pagan thought of sex in marriage as unholy, impure, and certainly as *not good*. The pagan indulged in sex, all right, often in perversions of sex. The temples of the pagan gods were, in effect, sordid houses of prostitution and debauchery of every kind in the name of "worship." But to the pagan mind, holiness and purity belonged to the people who had renounced sex forever—never to a married couple still engaging in the act of marriage.

Virginity became the symbol of spirituality, just as the Roman Vestal Virgins had represented ideal Virtue. At least three streams of philosophy totally foreign to the Word of God crept into the thinking of Christians and distorted the perspective of the church on the sacredness of married love for centuries to come.

First, the Greek Stoics, scorning human emotions, began the custom of allegorizing human passions in literature until human feelings became only pale symbols of "spiritual" concepts. This approach the church applied to the Song of Solomon. Second, the Greek philosopher, Plato, had taught that you could not have *both* earthly love and spiritual love; therefore, it was better to renounce the earthly and physical in hope of acquiring the spiritual. This view strongly influenced Christian teachers. Third, the Gnostic cults taught married couples to renounce all human sexuality in marriage in favor of a mystical "marriage" with the Spirit.

Obviously, the Song of Solomon contradicted these views and could not be tolerated by churchmen who held them unless its teachings were "spiritualized" so that the marriage described in the Song became only a symbol of mystical marriage with God.

Not surprisingly then, the church throughout the Middle Ages regarded celibacy as the greatest of virtues, and its teachers continued the attempt to turn the Song of Solomon with its joyous celebration of sacred married love into something else—a spiritualized allegory free from the "carnal taint" of human love in marriage. Only a few brave monks and an occasional bishop taught the Song in its plain sense as a work praising marriage and the dignity and purity of human love springing from God's love.

The holy beauty of wedded love was rediscovered by Christians in the sixteenth century when the Puritans and other reformers looked to the Bible as the final authority for doctrine and conduct. The Puritans unanimously declared that the sex drive was created by God and therefore was good in principle. And some of them pointed to the Song of Solomon as providing instruction in perfect married love.

Today the uninformed tend to tag Puritans as prudes—perhaps because they always insisted on the sacredness and privacy of sex in marriage and were appalled by sexual perversions just as the Bible is. But their attitudes toward sexual love between husband and wife were expressive, not repressive; positive, not negative; and both joyous and reverent. In *Paradise Lost*, the great Puritan poet, John Milton, hailed wedded love as a

> Perpetual fountain of domestic sweets,
> Whose bed is undefiled and chaste pronounced.

Unfortunately, the Victorian embarrassment with sex in the nineteenth century kept allegorical interpretations of the Song of Solomon in vogue. Those who saw the Song as plainly teaching the stages of true and chaste love in marriage were shouted down, sometimes by absurd arguments. For example, in a debate on the Song of Solomon, when Dr. J. Pye Smith showed the allegorical method to be "contrary to all the laws of language and reason and detrimental to real religion," Dr. James Bennett answered that there *had* to be an allegorical interpretation because "the language of the Song in its literal sense is contrary to the nature and modesty of women!"

We can better understand the basis for that remarkable statement by hearing what the medical expert on Victorian sexuality believed about women. In a book called *The Functions and Disorders of the Re-productive Organs*, Dr. William Acton asserted:

> The majority of women (happily for them) are not very much troubled with sexual feelings of any kind. . . . The best mothers, wives, and managers of households know little or nothing of sexual indulgences. Love of home, children, and domestic duties are the only passions they feel. . . . A modest women seldom desires any sexual gratification for herself.

For the past few decades the air has been clearing. Bible scholars have returned to the literal interpretation of the Song of Solomon as the foremost biblical teaching on love in marriage by example. It is now recognized as a carefully constructed unit with a clear message rather than (as some had said) an odd assortment of writings carelessly put together like sheet music stuck in a music rack. New scholarship is being directed to the understanding of the metaphors that make up the poetic imagery of the Song of Solomon. Nowhere can the fruits of this study be enjoyed more than in *A Song for Lovers* by S. Craig Glickman—an excellent book for you to use in your further study of the Song of Solomon.

Long ago the ''mysteries'' of Solomon's Song were likened to a lock for which the key had been lost. But, as Marvin H. Pope, Professor of Northwest Semitic Languages at Yale University, observes,

> The door to the understanding of the Song was not locked, nor even shut, but has been wide open to any who dared to see and enter. The barrier has been a psychological aversion to the obvious, somewhat like the Emperor's New Clothes. The trouble has been that interpreters who dared acknowledge the plain sense of the Song were assailed as enemies of truth and decency. . . . In recent decades there has been a general and growing tendency to reject allegory and freely admit the application of the Song to human physical love.[1]

As we consider the Song, we need to keep in mind the inspired view of the Hebrews who wrote the Old Testament. To them there was no real division between the love of God, the love of neighbor, and the sensuous love of husband and wife. In each case the same root word—*ahavah*—is used:

"You shall love (*ahavah*) the LORD your God" (Deuteronomy 6:5 NASB).

"You shall love (*ahavah*) your neighbor as yourself" (Leviticus 19:18 NASB).

"How fair and how pleasant art thou, O love (*ahavah*), for delights!" (Song of Solomon 7:6).

Love between husband and wife is seen as a Divine imperative, as the fulfillment of the will of God. The Song of Solomon teaches the searcher of its truths that romantic, sensual love is His gift and creation for marriage—that He honors and blesses true romantic love between husband and wife: therefore, love can be developed in one's marriage to the glory of God.

The very thing that offended and perplexed the Victorians such as Dr. Bennett is the characteristic that sets the Song apart from other poetry of its day. This is the total absence of male chauvinism and the equal role of the wife in the love affair. In the wisdom of the Holy Spirit, the book was written from the woman's viewpoint. This dramatically differs from other ancient oriental writings, according to Professor Chaim Rabin of the Hebrew University in Jerusalem. The bride (we will call her *Shulamith*, the feminine counterpart of Solomon, i.e., *Mrs. Solomon*) frankly expresses her longing for her husband in a way that reflects the reality of Genesis 3:16: "Unto the woman he said, I will greatly multiply thy sorrow and thy conception; in sorrow thou shalt bring forth children; and *thy desire shall be to thy husband*, and he shall rule over thee" (italics mine). But, as we will see, this desire is met with equal intensity by the husband. It is as if in a marriage rightly corresponding to God's design that part of the curse on mankind is reversed in the free interchange of love between husband and wife

If Shulamith is the central figure of the narrative, the husband (Solomon in the early years of his reign) is sensed and seen through her eyes as the strong, vital, attractive man who finds her working in the vineyards, woos her, wins her love, makes her his queen, and causes her love for him to deepen and intensify with the passing of time.

Briefly, let us consider how this man loved his wife. What were his "secrets"? The husband trying to follow New Testament admonitions in carrying out his role can find no better guidelines and examples of Ephesians 5 in action than those provided by Solomon in the Song of Solomon.

Shulamith, we are told, was a country girl, chastely brought up, but required by her stepbrothers to work in the vineyards so that her skin became deeply tanned in contrast to the elegant, pampered, white-skinned ladies of the court. She felt inferior, unworthy to be Solomon's queen, but her husband skillfully and lovingly built up her self-image. He did this first of all by praise. He sensitively praised her in the areas where she felt most insecure. He voiced appreciation of her physical appearance and her lovely character in specifics, not in vague generalities. He compared her with all other women so favorably that she could rest in the sureness that she pleased him as no other woman could. He told her, in fact, that she was flawless . . . perfect in his eyes . . . *altogether lovely*. He did not say this just when they were courting or on their wedding night. He continued to praise her in the maturity of their marriage.

Husband, your wife needs to hear these same things from your lips. Every wife needs to be praised for her beauty by her husband. It is this that will make her beautiful!

But more, is to be learned from this husband. He not only praised Shulamith; he also totally refrained from criticizing her. Never was there a word of criticism, not even when, perhaps, she deserved it. His words to her were always positive, and they bore fruit in the kind of loving, responsive wife she became.

His love and approval was not just a private matter. The king showed publicly his adoration and respect for his wife. In the royal banqueting house, his banner over her was love. In other words it became obvious to everyone that Shulamith was the most important person in his kingdom—to be honored, respected, and protected in every way. He treated her like a queen, and that is what she became in truth. At the same time he privately loved her in such a way that she could finally give herself completely to him, withholding nothing of her trust, her thoughts, and her love.

Husband, how do you treat your wife publicly? Do you open doors for her . . . seat her at the table . . . hold her coat for her? These small courtesies give honor to the wife as the more delicate vessel. After all, your wife cannot *see* your mental attitude toward her. You must show it by simple actions that display your love for her and your care and protective concern for her wellbeing. Is your love a banner over her when other people are present? Do you often look at her? Respond to her glances? Listen to her? Make her feel she is the most important person in *your* kingdom? If you want a queen for a wife, publicly treat her as one.

Of course, the marriage in the Song of Solomon had problems of adjustment as all marriages do. It is no sin and is not unusual to have natural differences with your mate. The test of emotional and spiritual maturity is how you work these problems out.

Let's take one example from the Song. Shulamith had difficulty in adjusting to Solomon's demanding schedule as chief of state. One night, perhaps when he had promised to come home early, he did not arrive until very late. By this time she may have been offended; at the least she was more concerned about her own comfort and schedule than about loving her husband. So she said she was not ready to see him, and she would not open her bedroom door to him.

Now observe how he handled the situation. Instead of making an issue of it, he quietly withdrew for a few hours to let her think it over. He left her alone, and gave her time to deal with her negative feelings. Please note that he did not rebuke her. Instead, he left a sign of his love for her at the door—a gift of rare perfume.

Because he had not reacted as an irate husband, but had behaved as a lover, his wife quickly realized that she was in the wrong and should correct her mistake. As soon as he withdrew she began to long for him and went out to look for him. When the two were together again, the husband reassured his wife with tender love words repeated from their wedding night. In other words, "I love you just as much as ever." And wrapped up in his love, unspoken, was instant forgiveness for her rejection of him.

Certainly it was necessary for Shulamith to learn to adjust to her husband's occupation. The same is true for all wives. The New Testament Scriptures tell the wife to adapt herself to her husband. Even though your husband is not a king, his calling should be as important to you as if he were a monarch. You should show a vital interest in his work, not just in his paycheck. You should respect what your husband does for a living and should be able to admire the way in which he does it.

I want you to consider how this wife loved her husband. It was by her response. Brought up as a chaste young woman, she now was free to delight in her husband's caresses, and she wholeheartedly, exquisitely responded to his lovemaking. Obviously, she thought much about her husband. Her thoughts were occupied with him even when they could not be together because of his duties. She respected his manly character and often expressed her admiration of him to others. When he complimented her, she responded with her own apt expressions of praise and left him in no doubt as to her feelings for him. She was thrilled by his touch at all times, eager for his embraces, and she let him know it. She enjoyed his company and planned delightful times for the two of them. She stored up delights for him—both new and old ways to please him.

To see how she blossomed in the security of his love, we can compare three statements she made. When she first fell in love with him, she said, "My beloved is mine and I am his" (2:16). Her possession of him was uppermost in her mind. But later in their relationship she said, "I am my beloved's and my beloved is mine" (6:3). Note that she reversed the order! Now his possession of her was more important. Finally, in the fullness of their love, she said, "I am my beloved's and his desire is toward me" (7:10). By this time she was so focused on him that she had forgotten about possessing him. She had lost herself in the greatness of his love, and she gloried only in his desire for her. It is here that we see the seeming reversal of the situation pronounced in Genesis 3:16, for the word in the original language translated *desire* in "his desire is for me" is the same word used in Genesis 3:16 to describe the woman's strong, often unreturned desire for her husband—a word used only three times in all of Scripture. Now, this desire has become mutual!

Husbands, I want you to especially consider this request that Solomon made of Shulamith. He said, "Let me see thy countenance, let me hear thy voice; for sweet is thy voice, and thy countenance is lovely" (2:14).

This speaks of a man who loved to look into his wife's eyes, who loved to talk with her and to hear what she had to say to him. No wonder she became completely secure in his love! As a result of this openness and communication between them, their relationship could grow and mature until it became many-faceted, expressing all the aspects of love that we have discussed in this book. He was her brother, lover, teacher, friend, companion, husband; she was equally everything to him. Their conversation, their lovemaking, their enjoyment in being together became even deeper and richer in quality.

It is interesting that at the end of the Song, the husband's last words were, "Let me hear your voice" (see 8:13). These were like the words he had first whispered to her when they were courting. Then he had compared her to a gentle dove hidden from him whose voice he wanted to hear so that he could come to know the inmost person of her heart. Now he still longed with the same intensity to grow in the knowledge of his fascinating wife. And his wife repeated her longing to make love to him. The romance of their marriage had only increased with the years! At the same time, their physical love-life had become better and better, nourishing their entire relationship.

No doubt their experience enabled Solomon to write so feelingly in Proverbs 5:18–19: "Rejoice in the wife of your youth. As a loving hind and a graceful doe, let her breasts satisfy you at all times; be exhilarated always with her love" (NASB).

At the conclusion of this chapter you can read Glickman's "Interpretive Paraphrase of the Song of Solomon" to see for yourself the ways this couple built their love for each other. You will note that physical caressing was an important aspect of their relationship, but that all the facets of love sparkled in this marriage like the many-sided reflections of a perfectly cut diamond.

Then I encourage you to study the Song of Solomon in several modern translations of the Bible, using *A Song for Lovers* as a guide, always noticing the delicacy of this couple's language of love and remembering that they chose certain metaphors to express their deepest feelings in a most vivid and memorable way.

It is important for you to share the Song with your marriage partner so that you both can be aware of the truth that the love relationship you experience is a part of your worship of God.

A high point of the Song comes in chapter 4 with the wedding night of the bride and groom after the wedding procession of chapter 3. The first verse of chapter 5 contains the joyous words of the husband after their lovemaking: "I have come into my garden, my sister, my bride; I have gathered my myrrh along with my balsam. I have eaten my honeycomb with my honey; I have drunk my wine with my milk" (NASB). The young husband is describing their love as a beautiful garden and as a wonderful feast he has celebrated.

Then another voice speaks—a mysterious voice. Who can it be? Wedding guests? On the wedding night? Hardly! Only One could be with the couple at this most intimate time and that must be God Himself, the Creator who had prepared this couple for their night of His design. It is God who is approving and affirming the love physically shared this night. As Glickman explains, "He takes pleasure in what has taken place. He is glad they have drunk deeply of the fountain of love. Two of his own have experienced love in all the beauty and fervor and purity that he intended for them."

God's words are: "Eat, O loved ones; drink and be drunk, O
Lovers" (Song of Solomon 5:1b). In other words, Continue to
enjoy the feast of love I have prepared for you!

When we study the Song of Solomon we begin to realize just
how fortunate we are to have this inspired pattern for our own
love-life. Now let it bless your marriage from this time forth. A
good way to begin is by reading the following paraphrase aloud
together preferably while sitting close to each other.

The Most Beautiful Love Song Ever Written

Shulamith's First Days in the Palace (1:2–11)

The King's fiancée, Shulamith, in soliloquy
How I wish he would shower me with kisses for his
exquisite kisses are more desirable than the finest wine.
The gentle fragrance of your cologne brings the en-
chantment of springtime. Yes, it is the rich fragrance of
your heart that awakens my love and respect. Yes, it is
your character that brings you admiration from every
girl of the court. How I long for you to come take me
with you to run and laugh through the countryside of
this kingdom. (You see, the King had brought me to
the kingdom's palace.)
Women of the court to the King
We will always be very thankful and happy because
of you, O King. For we love to speak of the inspiring
beauty of your love.
Shulamith in soliloquy
They rightly love a person like you, my King.
Shulamith to women of the court
I realize that that I do not display the fair and delicate
skin of one raised in the comfort of a palace. I am
darkened from the sun—indeed, as dark as the tents of

the humble desert nomads I used to work beside. But now I might say that I am also as dark as the luxurious drapery of the King's palace. Nevertheless, what loveliness I do have is not so weak that the gaze of the sun should make it bow its head in shame. And if the glare of the sun could not shame me, please know that neither will the glare of your contempt. I could not help it that my stepbrothers were angry with me and demanded that I work in the vineyard they had leased from the King. It was impossible for me to care for it and for the vineyard of my own appearance.

Shulamith to King

Please tell me, you whom I love so deeply, where you take your royal flock for its afternoon rest. I don't want to search randomly for you, wandering about like a woman of the streets.

Women of the court to Shulamith

If you do not know, O fairest among women, why not simply go ahead and follow the trail of the flocks, and then pasture your flock beside the shepherds' huts?

King to Shulamith

Your presence captivates attention as thoroughly as a single mare among a hundred stallions. And how perfectly your lovely jewelry and necklace adorn your lovely face.

Women of the court to Shulamith

We shall make even more elegant necklaces of gold and silver to adorn her face.

In a Palace Room (1:12–14)

Shulamith in soliloquy

While my King was dining at his table, my perfume refreshed me with its soothing fragrance. For my King is the fragrance and my thoughts of him are like a sachet of perfume hung around my neck, over my heart, continually refreshing me. How dear he is to me, as dear as

the delicate henna blossoms in the oasis of En-Gedi.
What joy I have found in that oasis!

In the Countryside (1:15–2:7)

King to Shulamith
You are so beautiful, my love. You are so beautiful.
Your soft eyes are as gentle as doves.

Shulamith to King
And you are handsome, my love, and so enjoyable. It's
so wonderful to walk through our home of nature together. Here the cool grass is a soft couch to lie upon,
to catch our breath and to gaze at the beams and raft-
ers of our house—the towering cedars and cypresses
all around. Lying here I feel like a rose from the valley
of Sharon, the loveliest flower in the valley.

King to Shulamith
Only the loveliest flower in the valley? No, my love. To
me you are like a flower among thorns compared with
any other woman in the world.

Shulamith to King
And you, my precious King, are like a fruitful apple tree
among the barren trees of the forest compared with all
the men in the world.

Shulamith in soliloquy
No longer do I labor in the heat of the sun. I find cool
rest in the shade of this apple tree. Nourishment from
its magical fruit brings me the radiant health only love
brings. And he loves me so much. Even when he
brings me to the great royal banquets attended by the
most influential people in this kingdom and beyond, he
is never so concerned for them that his love and his
care for me is not as plain as a royal banner lifted high
above my head.

How dear he is to me! My delightful peace in his love
makes me so weak from joy that I must rest in his arms
for strength. Yet such loving comfort makes me more

joyful and weaker still. How I wish he could lay me down beside him and embrace me! But how important it is I promise, with the gentle gazelles and deer of the countryside as my witnesses, not to attempt to awaken love until love is pleased to awaken itself.

On the Way to the Countryside (2:8–17)

Shulamith in soliloquy

I hear my beloved. Look! He is coming to visit. And he is as dashing as a young stag leaping upon the mountains, springing upon the hills. There he is, standing at the door, trying to peer through the window and peep through the lattice. At last he speaks.

King to Shulamith

Come, my darling, my fair one, come with me. For look, the winter has passed. The rain is over and gone. The blossoms have appeared in the land. The time of singing has come, and the voice of the turtledove has been heard in the land. The fig tree has ripened its figs, and the vines in blossom have given forth fragrance. Let us go, my darling, my lovely one; come along with me. O my precious, gentle dove. You have been like a dove in the clefts of the mountain rocks, in the hidden places along the mountain trails. Now come out from the hidden place and let me see you. Let me hear the coo of your voice. For your voice is sweet and you are as gracefully beautiful as a dove in flight silhouetted against a soft blue sky. My love, what we have together is a valuable treasure; it is like a garden of the loveliest flowers in the world. Let us promise each other to catch any foxes that could spoil our garden when now at long last it blossoms for us.

Shulamith in soliloquy

My beloved belongs to me and I belong to him—this tender King who grazes his flock among the lilies.

166

A Pattern for Lovers

Shulamith to the King

How I long for the time when all through the night, until the day takes its first breath and the morning shadows flee from the sun, that you, my beloved King, might be a gazelle upon the hills of my breasts.

Shulamith Waits for Her Fiancé (3:1–5)

Shulamith in soliloquy

How I miss the one I love so deeply. I could not wait to see him. I thought to myself, "I must get up and find him. I will get up now and look around the streets and squares of the city for him. Surely I'll be able to find this one I love so much." But I could not find him. When the night watchmen of the city found me, I immediately asked them if they had seen this one I loved so deeply. But they had not. Yet no sooner did I pass from them than I found my beloved. I held on and on and would not let him go until I could bring him to my home. I still held on until my fearful anxieties left me and I felt peaceful once again. How hard it is to be patient! You women of the court, we must promise ourselves, by the gazelles and deer of the field, not to awaken love until love is pleased to awaken itself.

The Wedding Day (3:6–11)

Poet

What can this be coming from the outskirts of the city like columns of smoke, perfumed clouds of myrrh and frankincense, clouds of the scented powders of the merchant? Look! It is the royal procession with Solomon carried upon his lavish couch by his strongest servants. And take a look at all those soldiers around it! That is the imperial guard, the sixty mightiest warriors in the entire kingdom. Each one is an expert with his weapon and valiant in battle. Yet now each one has a sword at his side only for the protection of the King and his bride. Look at the luxurious couch Solomon is carried on. He has had it made especially for this day. He made its frame from the best timber of Lebanon. Its posts are made of silver, its back of gold, and its seat of royal purple cloth. And do you see its delicate craftsmanship! It reflects the skill of the women of the court who gave their best work out of love for the King and his bride. Let us all go out and look upon King Solomon wearing his elegant wedding crown. Let us go out and see him on the most joyful day of his life.

The Wedding Night (4:1–5:1)

King to Shulamith

You are so beautiful, my love, you are so beautiful. Your soft eyes are as gentle as doves from behind your wedding veil. Your hair is as captivating as the flowing movement of a flock descending a mountain at sunset. Your full and lovely smile is as cheerful and sparkling as pairs of young lambs scurrying up from a washing. And only a thread of scarlet could have outlined your lips so perfectly. Your cheeks flush with the redness of the pomegranate's hue. Yet you walk with dignity and stand with the strength of a fortress. Your necklace sparkles like the shields upon the fortress tower. But your breasts are as soft and gentle as fawns grazing among lilies. And now at last, all through the night— until the day takes its first breath and the morning shadows flee from the sun—I will be a gazelle upon the hills of your perfumed breasts. You are completely and perfectly beautiful, my love, and flawless in every way. Now bring your thoughts completely to me, my love. Leave your fears in the far away mountains and rest in the security of my arms.

You excite me, my darling bride; you excite me with but a glance of your eyes, with but a strand of your necklace. How wonderful are your caresses, my beloved bride. Your love is more sweetly intoxicating than the finest wine. And the fragrance of your perfume is better than the finest spices. The richness of honey and milk is under your tongue, my love. And the fragrance of your garments is like the fragrance of the forests of Lebanon.

You are a beautiful garden fashioned only for me, my darling bride. Yes, like a garden kept only for me. Or like a fresh fountain sealed just for me. Your garden is overflowing with beautiful and delicate flowers of every scent and color. It is a paradise of pomegranates with luscious fruit, with henna blossoms and nard, nard and saffron, calamus and cinnamon with trees of frankincense, myrrh and aloes with all the choicest of spices. And you are pure as fresh water, yet more than a mere fountain. You are a spring for many gardens—a well of life-giving water. No, even more, you are like the fresh streams flowing from Lebanon which give life to the entire countryside.

Shulamith to King

Awake, O north wind, and come, wind of the south. Let your breezes blow upon my garden and carry its fragrant spices to my beloved. May he follow the enchanting spices to my garden and come in to enjoy its luscious fruit.

King to Shulamith

I have rejoiced in the richness of your garden, my darling bride. I have been intoxicated by the fragrance of your myrrh and perfume. I have tasted the sweetness of your love like honey. I have enjoyed the sweetness of your love like an exquisite wine and the refreshment of your love like the coolness of milk.

Poet to couple

Rejoice in your lovemaking as you would rejoice at a great feast, O lovers. Eat and drink from this feast to the fullest. Drink, drink and be drunk with one another's love.

A Problem Arises (5:2–6:3)

Shulamith in soliloquy

I was half asleep when I heard the sound of my beloved husband knocking gently upon the door of our palace chamber. He whispered softly, "I'm back from the countryside, my love, my darling, my perfect wife." My only answer was a mumbled, "I've already gone to sleep, my dear." After all, I had already prepared for bed. I had washed my face and put on my old nightgown.

But then my beloved gently opened the door and I realized I really wanted to see him. I had hesitated too long though. By the time I arose to open the door, he had already walked away, leaving only a gift of my favorite perfume as a reminder of his love for me. Deep within my heart I was reawakened to my love for him. It was just that the fatigue and distractions of the day had brought my hesitating response. I decided to try to find him. I threw on my clothes, went outside the palace and began to call out to him.

But things went from bad to worse. The night watchmen of the city mistook me for a secretive criminal sneaking about in the night. They arrested me in their customarily rough style, then jerking my shawl from my head they saw the face of their newly found suspect—a "great" police force we have!

O, you women of the court, if you see my beloved King, please tell him that I deeply love him, that I am lovesick for him.

Women of the court to Shulamith

What makes your husband better than any other, O fairest of women? What makes him so great that you request this so fervently of us?

Shulamith to women of the court

My beloved husband is strikingly handsome, the first to be noticed among ten thousand men. When I look at him, I see a face with a tan more richly golden than gold itself. His hair is as black as a raven's feathers and as lovely as palm leaves atop the stately palm tree. When I look into his eyes, they are as gentle as doves peacefully resting by streams of water. They are as pure and clear as health can make them.

When he places his cheek next to mine, it is as fragrant as a garden of perfumed flowers. His soft lips are as sweet and scented as lilies dripping with nectar. And how tender are his fingers like golden velvet when he touches me! He is a picture of strength and vitality. His stomach is as firm as a plate of ivory rippling with sapphires. And his legs are as strong and elegant as alabaster pillars set upon pedestals of fine gold. His appearance is like majestic Mt. Lebanon, prominent with its towering cedars.

But beyond all this, the words of his heart are full of charm and delight. He is completely wonderful in every way. This is the one I love so deeply, and this is the one who is my closest friend, O women of the palace court.

Women of the court to Shulamith
Where has your beloved gone, then, O fairest among women? Where has he gone? We will help you find him.

Shulamith to women of the court
Oh, I know him well enough to know where he has gone. He likes to contemplate as he walks through the garden and cares for his special little flock among the lilies. I know him, for I belong to him and he belongs to me—this gentle shepherd who pastures his flock among the lilies.

The Problem Resolved (6:4-13)

King to Shulamith
My darling, did you know that you are as lovely as the city of Tirzah glittering on the horizon of night? No,

more than that you are as lovely as the fair city of Jerusalem. Your beauty is as breathtaking as scores of marching warriors. (No, do not look at me like that now, my love; I have more to tell you.)

Do you remember what I said on our wedding night? It is still just as true. Your hair is as captivating as the flowing movement of a flock descending a mountain at sunset. Your lovely smile is as cheerful and sparkling as pairs of young lambs scurrying up from a washing. And your cheeks still flush with the redness of the pomegranate's hue.

King in soliloquy

The palace is full of its aristocratic ladies and dazzling mistresses belonging to the noblemen of the court. But my lovely wife, my dove, my flawless one, is unique among them all. And these ladies and mistresses realize it too. They too must praise her. As we approached them in my chariot, they eventually perceived that we were together again.

Women of the court to one another

Who is that on the horizon like the dawn, now fair as the moon but now plain and bright as the sun and as majestic as scores of marching warriors?

Shulamith in the chariot in soliloquy

I went down to the garden where I knew my King would be. I wanted to see if the fresh flowers and fruits of spring had come. I wanted to see if our reunion might bring a new season of spring love for my husband and me. Before I knew what happened, we were together again and riding past the palace court in his chariot. I can still hear them calling out, "Return, return O Shulamith; return that we may gaze at the beloved wife of the King."

King to Shulamith

How they love to look upon the incomparable grace and beauty of a queen.

172

In the Royal Bedroom (7:1-10)

King to Shulamith

How delicate are your feet in sandals, my royal prince's daughter! The curves of your hips are as smooth and graceful as the curves of elegant jewelry, perfectly fashioned by the skillful hands of a master artist. As delectable as a feast of wine and bread is your stomach—your navel is like the goblet of wine, and your stomach is the soft warm bread. Your breasts are as soft and gentle as fawns grazing among lilies, twins of a gazelle, and your neck is smooth as ivory to the touch. Your eyes are as peaceful as the pools of water in the valley of Heshbon, near the gate of the populous city.

Yet how strong you walk in wisdom and discretion. You are, indeed, as majestically beautiful as Mt. Carmel. Your long flowing hair is as cool and soft as silken threads draped round my neck, yet strong enough to bind me as your captive forever. How lovely and delightful you are, my dear, and how especially delightful is your love! You are as graceful and splendrous as a palm tree silhouetted against the sky. Yes, a palm tree—and your breasts are its luscious fruit.

I think I shall climb my precious palm tree and take its tender fruit gently into my hand. O my precious one, let your breasts be like the tender fruit to my taste, and now let me kiss you and breathe your fragrant breath. Let me kiss you and taste a sweetness better than wine.

Shulamith to King

And savor every drop, my lover, and let its sweetness linger long upon your lips, and let every drop of this wine bring a peaceful sleep.

Shulamith in soliloquy

I belong to my beloved husband and he loves me from the depths of his soul.

In the Countryside (7:11–8:14)

Shulamith to King

Spring's magic flowers have perfumed the pastel countryside and enchanted the hearts of all lovers. Come,
my precious lover; every delicious fruit of spring is ours
for the taking. Let us return to our springtime cottage of
towering cedars and cypresses where the plush green
grass is its endless carpet and the orchards are its
shelves for every luscious fruit. I have prepared a bas-
ketful for you, my love, to give you in a sumptuous
banquet of love beneath the sky.

I wish we could pretend you were my brother, my
real little brother. I could take you outside to play, and
playfully kiss you whenever I wished. But then I could
also take your hand and bring you inside and you
could teach me and share with me your deep understanding of life. Then how I wish you would lay me
down beside you and love me.

Shulamith to women of the court

I encourage you not to try to awaken love until love is
pleased to awaken itself. How wonderful it is when it
blossoms in the proper season.

Shulamith to King

Do you remember where our love began? Under the
legendary sweetheart tree, of course, where every love
begins and grows and then brings forth a newborn
child, yet not without the pain of birth. Neither did our
love begin without the pain, the fruitful pain of birth. O,
my darling lover, make me your most precious possession held securely in your arms, held close to your
heart. True love is as strong and irreversible as the onward march of death. True love never ceases to care,
and it would no more give up the beloved than the
grave would give up the dead.

The fires of true love can never be quenched because the source of its flame is God himself. Even were a river of rushing water to pass over it, the flame would yet shine forth. Of all the gifts in the world, this priceless love is the most precious and possessed only by those to whom it is freely given. For no man could purchase it with money, even the richest man in the world.

King to Shulamith

Do you remember how it was given to us?

Shulamith to King

My love, I truly believe I was being prepared for it long before I even dreamed of romance. I remember hearing my brothers talking one evening. It was shortly after my father died, and they were concerned to raise me properly, to prepare me for the distant day of marriage. They were like a roomful of fathers debating about what to do with their only daughter. They finally resolved simply to punish and restrict me if I were promiscuous but to reward and encourage me if I were chaste. How thankful I am that I made it easy for them. I could see even when I was very young that I wanted to keep myself for the one dearest man in my life.

And then you came. And everything I ever wanted I found in you. There I was, working daily in the vineyard my brothers had leased from you. And you "happened" to pass by and see me. That's how our love began.

I remember when I worked in that vineyard that a thousand dollars went to you and two hundred dollars for the ones taking care of its fruit for you. Now I am your vineyard, my lover, and I gladly give the entire thousand dollars of my worth to you; I give myself completely, withholding nothing of my trust, my thoughts, my care, my love. But my dear King, let us not forget that two hundred dollars belongs to the ones who took care of the fruit of my vineyard for you. How thankful we must be to my family who helped prepare me for you.

King to Shulamith

My darling, whose home is the fragrant garden, everyone listens for the sound of your voice, but let me alone hear it now.

Shulamith to King

Hurry, then, my beloved. And again be like a gazelle or young stag on the hills of my perfumed breasts.*

*Taken from *A Song for Lovers* by S. Craig Glickman. © 1976 by Inter-Varsity Christian Fellowship of the USA and used by permission of InterVarsity Press.

13

Prescription for a Superb Marriage

If you have read and absorbed the love-life principles we have discussed up to this point, you are ready for my prescription for a superb marriage.

The prescription involves a practical course of action for husband and wife that is both uncomplicated and effective. You will be able to remember it readily because it is called the B-E-S-T, an acronym representing the four positive elements that will transform any marriage. These are not steps to be tried one at a time, but four measures to be taken simultaneously and maintained consistently. If necessary, they can be implemented by either partner alone. In many cases, one of you will have to make the first move without any promise of cooperation from the other. So, if you want the best marriage possible with the mate you have chosen, then give your partner the *best*:

> B *lessing*
> E *difying*
> S *haring*
> T *ouching*

1) Blessing

Perhaps you have never thought of blessing as a practical element to be introduced into marriage. The principle of blessing is a biblical one, and the Christian is commanded to practice it, most particularly in response to annoyance or provocation. Learning this important technique of response will carry you through the difficult moments that occur in any marriage and will bring peace to the troubled waters of your relationship. The practice of blessing puts an end to the volley of sharp words that mars so many love affairs, and that is only the beginning of its benefits for you.

The word *"blessing"* in the New Testament *(eulogia)* is based on two Greek words: *eu*, meaning "well," and *logos*, meaning "word." The first way of blessing your marriage partner is to speak well of him or her, and to respond with good words even when your partner's speech becomes harsh, critical, or insulting. The Lord Jesus gave us an example we are advised to follow: when He was reviled, He did not revile in return, and when He suffered, He uttered no threats, but kept entrusting Himself to His Father in heaven. *In the same way*, Scripture says, we are to live as husbands and wives. The wife described in Proverbs 31 receives praise because she opens her mouth in wisdom and the law of kindness is on her tongue. James warns us about the inconsistency of sending forth both blessing and cursing from our mouth as if we were a fountain pouring out a mixture of fresh and bitter water. And Peter tells us that if we love life and want to see "good days," we will keep our tongue from speaking evil in any form.

To put this in the most practical terms, you have the power to bless your marriage by the words you speak to your partner. You can also bless by learning when to be silent.

Three other aspects of blessing are found in Scripture. You bless by bestowing practical benefits upon; simply by doing kind things for another person. When is the last time you did something kind for your mate just to please, not as a duty, but as a gift of blessing? This should be a daily part of your marriage.

You also bless by showing thankfulness and appreciation. Whatever you can find to appreciate in your partner, make it known verbally. Thank your partner and thank God too.

Finally, you bless by calling God's favor down in prayer. How much are you praying for your partner? And on what basis? So things will be easier for you? Or is it prayer for your partner's good and blessing?

To sum up, you bless your partner and your marriage in these four ways: (1) through your good and loving words spoken to him and about him; (2) through your practical behavior, which shows loving kindness toward him in actions large and small; (3) through conveying your attitude of thankfulness and appreciation for him; (4) through your prayer to God on his behalf. Good words . . . kind actions . . . thankful appreciation . . . and intercessory prayer for your partner.

Blessing in its fullness will work wonders when applied to your marriage. No matter how your partner treats you, blessing should be your response. Scripture tells us that the Lord protects and honors the husband or wife who applies biblical principles all the time. You have been promised good days as a result of giving blessing. The Lord has promised to protect you and hear your prayers. And, when blessing your partner, you take yourself out of the way so that the Lord is free to work in the life of the partner who may be rendering evil.

If all of this helps a troubled marriage, think of how a good marriage can be enhanced when two people begin to bless each other!

2) Edifying

Edifying, a biblical term often used in the New Testament, refers to the building up of individuals. Although Christians can be edified spiritually by preaching, I do not recommend this means of edifying your marriage partner. When I suggested to one wife that she begin to edify her husband, she said, startled, "Do you mean I am supposed to *preach* to him?"

I quickly assured her that preaching was not what I had in mind; that by edifying, I meant building her husband up in every aspect of his personality, cheering him on in every area of life, and increasing his sense of self-worth with the result that his capacity to love and give of himself would be increased as well.

179

Elizabeth Barrett Browning expressed the principle of edifying in a few succinct words when she wrote to the man she would marry, "Make thy love larger to enlarge my worth." When we speak of edifying, we are referring to an expanded love expressed in positive ways that enlarges the self-worth of the beloved. You see, this is a great gift that you can give to your partner.

We can appreciate the psychological connotations of edifying by considering the root meaning of the word. The English word *edify* goes back to an old Latin word *aedes,* which originally meant a hearth or fireplace. A fireplace has emotional associations for most of us, representing cozy warmth, loving togetherness, and, perhaps, a special tranquillity. The hearth was the center of activity in ancient times, the only place of warmth and light in the home, and the place where the daily bread was prepared. Certainly it was the place where people were drawn together, comforted, and sustained in the midst of the harsh realities of life.

In today's marriage, the process of edifying holds a similar place of importance in the emotional sense. We find as we study the New Testament passages that speak of edifying that three golden strands are interwoven: personal encouragement, inner strengthening, and the establishment of peace and harmony between individuals. For example:

"So let us then definitely aim for and eagerly pursue what makes for harmony and for mutual upbuilding (edification and development) of one another" (Romans 14:19 AMPLIFIED).

"Let each one of us make it a practice to please (make happy) his neighbor for his good and for his true welfare, to edify him—that is, to strengthen him and build him up spiritually" (Romans 15:2 AMPLIFIED).

"Therefore encourage one another and build each other up, just as in fact you are doing" (1 Thessalonians 5:11 NIV).

1 Corinthians 8:1 sums up the matter of edifying: "Love builds up" (NIV).

But how do you build up your mate? A careful study of New Testament principles and the example of the Song of Solomon indicates that husbands and wives each have their own ways of edifying. In brief, the husband edifies his wife by praising her. The wife edifies her husband by her loving response to him.

Husbands are commanded in Ephesians 5 to nourish and cherish their wives. This is at least partially accomplished through the giving of verbal praise and encouragement. A wife's sense of her own beauty depends greatly on what her husband thinks of her. She needs to be nourished emotionally with praise and never diminished by criticism, especially in the areas where she feels most insecure and vulnerable. She needs to be cherished in public, and the test of this is how her husband treats her socially. You can be sure that a genuinely beautiful wife has been protected and cherished by a husband who has shown a sensitive response to her special needs.

Remember, edification builds up, never tears down. So love gives your partner freedom to grow and develop as a person without fear of failure and fear of hurtful criticism.

Some husbands who manage to refrain from criticism still have not learned the art of praise for their wives. It is said, "The best way to compliment your wife is *frequently*." On the other hand, relationships die because of what you *don't* say. They simply dry up!

Edifying begins in the thought life where Philippians 4:8 is applied: "If there is any excellence and if anything worthy of praise, let your mind dwell on these things" (NASB). Practice thinking about things you find attractive in your mate—every positive quality your partner possesses. Let the words of your lips be governed by this principle: Will these words build up or tear down? Then ask yourself: What can I say to my partner right now that will edify and build up, encourage, strengthen, and bring peace?

Biblically, the wife best edifies her husband by her response to him. In the full meaning of the language of the Greek New Testament, the wife is told to respect, admire, be in awe of, defer to, revere, adore, esteem, praise, and deeply love her husband. This is presented as her full-time job, and the original language of

181

the Bible indicates that she will be personally benefited as she does it.

God has designed marriage so that a husband is dependent on the affirmations of his wife, the appreciation she shows him for all that he gives her, and her demonstration of respect for his manhood. It is wounding when a husband criticizes his wife. It is equally wounding when the wife criticizes what her husband provides for her.

Both husband and wife have a tremendous need for encouragement by word, by focused attention, by eye contact, and by loving touch to keep them alive as growing, confident individuals. Psychologists call this *healing attention*. We call it *edifying*.

The New Testament Greek word for "edify" reminds us of an important fact. It is *oikodomeo*, a combination of two words: *oikos*, meaning a family, home, or house, and *demo*, meaning to build. While you are edifying and building each other up, you also are building a home together. Your home can never be what it should be until you have developed the practice of edifying. Let it begin with you!

3) Sharing

We have already discussed this third element in building a superb marriage. You may wish to refer again to chapters 9 and 11. I would like to reemphasize several points. The more ways you can find to be in relationship with each other, the stronger your love will become. Sharing should touch all areas of life—your time, activities, interests and concerns, ideas and innermost thoughts, spiritual walk, family objectives and goals, etc.

Sharing demands giving of yourself, listening to your partner, and, as you live life together, developing a sensitive awareness of moments that offer possibilities for deepening the love between you.

Picture it as taking an adventurous voyage of discovery together, for you will be discovering interesting new territory in each other through the experience of sharing on successively deeper levels.

Yes, this too is a biblical principle. Husband and wife are to become *one* flesh. The Book of Acts tells us that all the believers were *one* in heart and soul and, at that time, even had their possessions in common. If this sharing could happen within a group of people, how much more possible it is to develop oneness of heart and soul between two people who want to build love in their marriage!

4) Touching

If you have read this book carefully up to this point, you already know how essential physical touching is to every human being. God created us with hundreds of thousands of microscopic nerve endings in our skin designed to sense and benefit from a loving touch. A tender touch tells us that we are cared for. It can calm our fears, soothe pain, bring us comfort, or give us the blessed satisfaction of emotional security. As adults, touching continues to be a primary means of communicating with those we love, whether we are conscious of it or not. Our need for a caring touch is normal and healthy and we will never outgrow it.

But if touching is so valuable and pleasurable, why is it necessary to advise couples to do more of it? The answer lies in our culture. While our western civilization is highly sexual, it frowns on or ignores touching apart from sex. This is particularly true for men, for there are only three acceptable kinds of touching in today's world: the superficial handshake, aggressive contact sports, and the sexual encounter. Men have been conditioned to turn to sex whenever they feel any need for loving closeness. No wonder experts believe that our extreme preoccupation with sex in this society is actually an expression of our deep, unsatisfied need for the warmth, reassurance, and intimacy of nonsexual touching.

Those of you who begin to practice physical touching in your marriage in all of its pleasant nonsexual forms will find that you may be having sex a little less often, but enjoying it much more. Snuggling and cuddling, sleeping close to each other, sharing affection through simple touch, will meet many of the emotional needs that you hoped sex would provide. At the same time, this pattern of affectionate closeness provides a delightful prelude to the entire sex relationship, preparing the way emotionally for wonderful times together.

I must emphasize that even though you apply every other principle I have given you in this book, it will be of little avail unless you learn to touch each other often and joyfully in nonsexual ways. Physical contact is absolutely essential in building the emotion of love. You may take it as a sobering warning that most of the time marital infidelity is not so much a search for sex as it is for emotional intimacy. The Scriptures indicate that touching a woman kindles a flame that should be natural within marriage. If you would like to kindle a flame in your own marriage, then begin to show your love through physical touching.

Blessing . . . Edifying . . . Sharing . . . Touching . . . a four-point prescription for a superb marriage! But prescriptions are useful only when taken as directed. As a family doctor, I find that some of my patients do not take their prescriptions or do not follow the directions on them. At their next visit, when there has been no improvement, the truth comes out.

In your own case, if you add these four elements to your marriage according to directions, you will soon see a dramatic improvement. I often hear these words from a happy husband or wife: "It works! The B-E-S-T really works!"

To be sure you are applying these principles correctly, I want to give you some additional helps in each area. This time we will begin with the simplest of the four elements—touching—and conclude with the more challenging part of the prescription—blessing.

Twenty-Five Suggestions for Touching

1. When dating, young people can scarcely be kept apart. Most married couples have forgotten how much fun physical closeness can be! So set aside practice times at night (at least once a week) to learn the delights of nonsexual body caressing. Make a date ahead of time. Anticipate pleasure and relaxation together.

2. Show each other where you like to be touched and the kind of touch that pleases you. Usually, a light touch is the most thrilling. Be imaginative in the way you caress.
3. Remember the purpose: to establish a good emotional climate of warmth, love, and affection; *not* to initiate sex. If sex results later because you both want it, that's all right. But you need to learn to enjoy *nonsexual* touching during these exercise times.
4. Demonstrate to each other how you prefer to be held. Kiss your partner the way you would like to be kissed—not to criticize past performances, but to communicate something your partner has not sensed before.
5. Use lotion or baby oil in body caressing; use K-Y Jelly when touching the more sensitive areas of the body. Physical caressing should be totally pleasant.
6. Try caressing (not tickling!) each other's feet. For almost everyone this is a pleasurable and nonthreatening form of touch communication. Some people bathe, dry, and oil each other's feet gently and leisurely.
7. Cleanliness is essential for enjoyment of these sessions.
8. Some evenings take your shower or bath together. Make this a lighthearted, sensuous experience.
9. Americans habitually do everything in a rush, including lovemaking. But to learn the art of expressing warm, sensual feelings, you will have to slow down. If what you are doing feels good, take the time to enjoy it. This may become the best part of your day.
10. Caress each other's back. Pay special attention to the back of the neck at the hairline and the area just above the small of the back.
11. Maintain a positive attitude (the attitude of yes, rather than no). If some manner of caressing or the area chosen does not feel particularly enjoyable, gently lead your partner on to something you do like. Never say, "Stop doing that!" or similar words. The atmosphere should be delightfully permissive.

12. Practice communicating warmth. Learn to be emotionally aware of your own feelings and those of your partner. Focus on expressing your love through the medium of touch. Caress each other's face in the dark, becoming more aware of your partner and spelling out love through sensitive fingertips.
13. Make sure that both of you are having equal opportunity to give and to receive. Take turns giving pleasure to each other.
14. When you caress, use a slow, tender, appreciative touch, indicating how much you enjoy your partner's body—each part of it. When people feel negative about some part of their body, it is more difficult for them to relate freely to their partner. Help your mate realize that every part of his or her body is pleasing, attractive, and desirable to you.
15. Develop positive feelings toward your own body given to you by God. This is biblical! Meditate on Psalm 139. "I praise you because I am fearfully and wonderfully made; your works are wonderful, I know that full well" (Psalm 139:14 NIV).
16. Communicate verbally during your exercises, telling each other what you especially enjoy and how it makes you feel.
17. Sleep in as few clothes as possible at night. Clothes are only a hindrance during these touching sessions.
18. Practice breathing together in rhythm, both of you lying on your side, the other pressed up against your back, hand on your abdomen to gauge your breathing and adjust his rhythm to yours. Then reverse places and do it again.
19. Try to go to bed when your partner does *every* night.
20. Have a period of fifteen to thirty minutes every night to lie in each other's arms in the dark before you drift off to sleep. Whisper together, sharing private thoughts and pleasant little experiences of the day. Avoid controversial or negative topics. This is the time to build intimacy and wind down for sleep. You will become used to sharing things with each other that you would not otherwise mention. In each other's arms the hurts and frustrations of the day are healed. You may want to pray together at this time, or just relax in the comfort of physically-felt love.

186

21. Establish the cozy habit of staying in some sort of physical contact while you are going to sleep—a hand or a leg touching your partner's, for instance.

22. Begin every day with a few minutes of cuddling and snuggling before you get out of bed. A husband can tell his wife how nice she feels and how glad he is to be close to her. A wife can nestle in her husband's arms and tell him she wishes they didn't have to leave each other that morning. Just be close and savor gentle physical contact for awhile. It will make the morning bout with the alarm clock far more pleasant, so allow a few minutes in your schedule for this, even though one or both of you must soon be up and off to work.

23. Hold hands often. Think of all the different ways you can enjoy just touching with your hands, and all the different feelings that can be conveyed.

24. Become aware of the many ways you can have physical contact in the course of a week. Touch when you are talking and maintain eye contact. Sit close to each other in church. Kiss each other when there is no occasion for it. Add variety to your kisses, your touches, and your love pats.

25. While you watch television, make sure you sit close together and use the time for some physical communication. A wise wife will cuddle close to her husband when he chooses to watch his football games, even if she is not interested in the program. Since so many people spend so much time before the TV set, it need not be wasted if they are at least together physically.

My final word on touching: even if you practice everything else in this book, but do not touch each other frequently and lovingly, the thrill of romantic love will be absent from your marriage. It's up to you to add the spark.

A Creative View of Sharing

1. Take another look at *sharing* through the eyes of two lovers whose love endured:

We talked deeply . . . about justice between lovers and about how to make love endure. What emerged from our talk was nothing less, we believed, than the central "secret" of enduring love: sharing.

"Look," we said, "what is it that draws two people into closeness and love? Of course there's the mystery of physical attraction, but beyond that it's the things they share. We both love strawberries and ships and collies and poems and all beauty, and all those things bind us together. Those sharings just happened to be; but what we must do now is share *everything*. Everything! If one of us likes *anything,* there must be something to like in it—and the other one must find it. Every single thing that either of us likes. That way we shall create a thousand strands, great and small, that will link us together. Then we shall be so close that it would be impossible— unthinkable—for either of us to suppose that we could ever recreate such closeness with anyone else. And our trust in each other will not only be based on love and loyalty but on the *fact* of a thousand sharings—a thousand strands twisted into something unbreakable."

Our enthusiasm grew as we talked. Total sharing, we felt, was the ultimate secret of a love that would last forever. And of course we *could* learn to like anything if we wanted to. Through sharing we would not only make a bond of incredible friendship, but through sharing we would keep the magic of inloveness. And with every year, more and more depth. We would become as close as two human beings *could* become— closer perhaps than any two people have ever been. Whatever storms might come, whatever changes the years might bring, there would be the bedrock closeness of all our sharing. [1]

2. Now, creatively evaluate where you can develop sharing in your own marriage. Look at your life together in these four areas:

   - *Common Ground.* Think of all the things you actually share right now. How can you enjoy it more?
   - *Separate Ground.* Parts of your life, particularly in the area of work and responsibility, may be separate. You

188

may also have special interests that your partner will never become directly involved in. How can you bridge these gaps in order to share your separate worlds? Through communication? Through mutual understanding and encouragement?

- *New Ground for One*. What interests can you begin to enjoy because your partner enjoys them? If you each develop new enthusiasms to match your partner's, life will become more interesting than ever.
- *New Ground for Both*. What new, absorbing interests can you develop together?

The above should jog your own thinking as you plan creatively for more meaningful sharing in your marriage. Here's how Rich and Celia, a couple married four years, revised their approach to sharing:

"We had to start by admitting there were some segments of our personalities that would never quite mesh," Rich said. "I enjoy running a mile or two a day—the hotter the sun, the better. Cele likes to curl up in the shade with a book of poetry. I do a lot of heavy reading, while she's into crafts of all sorts. I'm a research scientist, and she's a second-grade school teacher. But we can share even our differences through conversation. We're beginning to communicate a lot more about the work and interests that we each have. And we're becoming more consciously proud of each other. Cele makes some beautiful art objects, and I insist that we use them in our home. I know she respects the work I do in meteorology and I tell her about it because she always seems interested. On the other hand, she brings her problems home from the classroom, and we discuss the best way to handle them. We often pray together for the children she's concerned about. It's amazing how close two people can become through sharing their separate worlds."

"I've become excited about photography," Cele said, "because it's one of Rich's favorite hobbies. He's taught me so much, and it satisfies my need to be creative. In the process, I've done a lot of strenuous hiking with him because we like to photograph the beauty of the mountain trails. Now we're learning something new together—cross-country skiing! Another world we're exploring together is classical music."

"This winter Cele suggested that we read *The Lord of the Rings* trilogy by J. R. R. Tolkien together—a chapter a night," Rich said. "It was a great idea sharing the pleasure of those books with each other."

"Rich never cared much for table games," Cele smiled, "but he's learned to play them because I enjoy them."

"And Cele has returned the favor by cooperating with me in organizing our financial affairs into a definite system that takes a lot of record-keeping," Rich added. "Now we do the housework and yardwork together instead of separately and talk while we're working. Sharing gets to be a habit—a nice habit. The more you do it, the more you want to."

Every couple's plan for sharing will be different. Just make sure you have a plan. The natural tendency is to go your separate ways. Sharing helps to create an *enduring* love.

Nine Ways to Edify

1. Make the irrevocable decision to never again be critical of your partner in word, thought, or deed. This may sound like an impossibility, but it is not. It is simply a decision backed up by action until it becomes a habit you would not change if you could.
2. Study your partner. Become sensitive to the areas where your partner feels a lack and think of ways to build up your partner in those areas particularly.
3. Think every day of positive qualities and behavior patterns you admire and appreciate in your mate.
4. Consistently verbalize praise and appreciation for your partner. Be genuine, be specific, be generous. You edify with the *spoken* word.
5. Recognize your partner's talents, abilities, and accomplishments. Communicate your respect for the work he or she does.

190

6. Husband, show your wife publicly and privately how precious she is to you. And do not express admiration for another woman. This is never edifying to your wife. Keep your attention focused on her!
7. Wife, show your husband that he is the most important person in your life—always. Seek his opinions and value his judgment.
8. Respond to each other physically and facially. The face is the most distinctive and expressive part of a person. Your mate wants to see you smile, eyes sparkling in response to him or her.
9. Always exhibit the greatest courtesy to each other. You should be VIPs in your own home!

Scriptural Counsel on Blessing

Do not repay evil with evil or insult with insult, but with blessing, because to this you were called so that you may inherit a blessing. For,

"Whoever would love life
and see good days
must keep his tongue from evil
and his lips from deceitful speech.
He must turn from evil and do good;
he must seek peace and pursue it.
For the eyes of the Lord are on the righteous,
and his ears are attentive to their prayer,
but the face of the Lord is against those
who do evil."   (1 Peter 3:9–12 NIV)

This New Testament Scripture with the passage quoted by Peter from Psalm 34:13–17 is very plain. God has called every Christian into a lifestyle of consistent blessing of others through (1) *words;* (2) *behavior.* This means consistently blessing those in our own household—our marriage partner first of all. Blessing in word and action is most especially required of us in response to any manner of evil behavior or insulting speech. As you apply this to your own marriage, understand that you never have any justification for speaking to your partner scornfully, angrily, or deceitfully. Your partner's bad behavior can never excuse your own in God's eyes. If you fail to bless, God says that your mouth will bring more trouble on you; you will miss out on the blessing that He had planned for you; and, instead, His face will be against you (i.e., nothing you try to do in your marriage will prosper).

The rewards of blessing are also plainly spelled out: God will see to it that we are blessed by Him (no matter what our partner does); that we will "love life" and experience good days; that He will watch over us with special protective care; and that He will hear and answer our prayers.

Few choices of life have been given to us more clearly. Often we hesitate between this path and that, wondering what the outcome will be. In this case, we know. If we choose the disciplined path of blessing in our marriage (the road surely less traveled by!), it will make all the difference in our life. We know it because God has said it.

The way is simple, if challenging, and can be followed by anyone who uses the spiritual resources the Lord Jesus Christ provides. Here are the directions.

Negatives:
(1) Keep your tongue from evil and your lips from speaking deceitful words.
(2) Turn away from evil.

Positives:
(1) Do good.
(2) Seek peace and pursue it.

More detailed counsel can be found in Romans 12:

"Bless those who persecute you; bless and do not curse. Rejoice with those who rejoice; mourn with those who mourn. Live in harmony with one another. Do not be proud, but be willing to associate with people of low position. Do not be conceited.

Do not repay anyone evil for evil. Be careful to do what is right in the eyes of everybody. If it is possible, as far as it depends on

192

you, live at peace with everyone. Do not take revenge, my friends, but leave room for God's wrath, for it is written: "It is mine to avenge; I will repay," says the Lord. On the contrary:
"If your enemy is hungry, feed him;
  If he is thirsty, give him something to drink.
In doing this, you will heap burning coals on his head."
Do not be overcome by evil, but overcome evil with good.

(Romans 12:14–21 NIV)

In short:

- Bless and do not curse the one who is giving you a hard time.
- Be empathic and understanding with your partner.
- Live in harmony with your mate.
- Do not think you are better than your partner.
- Do not act proud; do not act conceited.
- Do not repay evil with evil (even in the most petty detail).
- Be careful to do what your partner considers to be right.
- As far as it depends on you, live at peace in your marriage.
- Never take revenge.
- Consistently do kind things for your partner, no matter what treatment you receive.
- Do not let yourself be overcome by evil. Instead, overcome evil with good!

14

Removing the Barriers

One of our American generals made a profound observation about war. He said, "The only way to *win* a war is to prevent it."

As a marriage counselor, I recall these words when I work with couples who are at open war. No one is winning. No one *can* win. But the hostilities go on——husband and wife treating each other like bitter enemies!

In other marriages, hostilities exist under the surface, just as real even if semi-concealed. In the long run they will be equally deadly unless they are recognized and checked in time.

Let me ask you a personal question. Are there hostilities in your marriage, standing between you and the happiness you long for? Occasionally I counsel couples where either husband or wife will not admit to any bad feelings. They claim they feel nothing but indifference. Only after deeper consideration do they realize that their indifference is the direct result of buried anger that has led to depression, numbing all of their emotions, both happy and unhappy ones. It is important to understand that a negative attitude represents psychic energy that cannot be ignored or hidden away. This psychic energy is a force that must be reckoned with. When one tries either to maintain it or conceal it, so much emotional strength is required that the individual ends up drained and therefore very depressed.

We have been describing the incomparable joy experienced by husband and wife who learn to love each other with the fullness of love—*agape*, romance, belonging, cherished friendship, and physical fulfillment blended into a wonderful, enduring intimacy.

Now we must warn that this love cannot grow in the same heart with negative attitudes and bad feelings—anger, bitterness, resentment, pride, disillusionment, despair, or hostility (veiled or otherwise). Facing these and dealing with them in your own life will not only prevent a disastrous war, but can open up the way to a host of blessings. Not the least of these may be a love affair you no longer thought possible in your marriage.

We are going to concentrate only on *your* attitudes, not those of your partner. As you change for the better, this will inevitably have its effect on your mate.

I would like for you to visualize your negative attitudes as barriers obstructing the passage that leads to a genuine love relationship. Barriers separate and keep apart; they hinder and impede progress. But they are not *necessarily impassable*. So, if negative attitudes have taken root in your heart, I want to help you face them and remove them so that the way will be clear for the interchange of love. These attitudes go by different names because people react differently. One wife confessed to me that she was so angry with her husband that she had a desire to smother him as he slept, while another retreated into an icy resentment that caused her to say that now she could not respond to her husband even if he were perfect!

Whatever name you give to *your* negative attitudes, the common denominator will always be the same—an unforgiving spirit that can rob you of all that makes life good if you let it continue.

"But, Dr. Wheat, I am justified in my feelings," a husband or wife sometimes protests. "You don't know how I've been treated!"

My answer is that this is not the issue. You personally are faced with a choice. Let me spell it out so that you can make a conscious, rational decision. Otherwise you will slide into a choice almost unconsciously, a decision based on emotion with neither logic nor the Word of God to back it up.

If you want a marriage full of love, you cannot afford the

luxury of resentment or self-pity or anger. Unforgiveness toward your mate in any form (including the self-protective shield of distrust) will be the death blow to love. If you choose to cling to your bad feelings, they will cripple your marriage relationship and at the same time they will take their toll of your physical health and emotional well-being.

Of course, all normal people want health and happiness and love in their marriage. But they often do not know how to handle the past; how to deal with their negative attitudes; how to cope with their resentments; or how to recognize their own anger buried under a layer of depression. Many do not know how to forgive, and they think it must be very complicated or even impossible. But it is not. God never asks His children to do anything that He does not provide both the instructions for and the strength to accomplish.

Let me share two basic principles that will help you at this point. First, *you do not have to be controlled by your feelings*. Second, *you are not the helpless prisoner of your past*.

These are the chief objections people offer when told they need to forgive. Their answer goes like this . . . "Maybe so, but I can never *feel* any forgiveness toward my husband after what he *did*." Or, "I'd like to forgive my wife, but I can't change the way *I feel. I can't change the past*." These people are confessing a state of slavery. They are picturing themselves as enslaved by their own feelings, as prisoners of events that happened in the past. And yet Christians have already been set free! Jesus said, "You will know the truth, and the truth will set you free. . . . If the Son sets you free, you will be free indeed" (John 8:32, 36 NIV). If you are a Christian, trusting in Jesus Christ alone for your salvation, right now you are more free than you know!

Even in the secular world counselors are dramatically changing their approach in a way that is much more in accord with biblical principles. Counselors no longer give exclusive attention to the patient's *feelings;* many of them now concentrate on the importance of the individual's *behavior*. The most effective counselors no longer attempt prolonged treatment of the patient's past; instead, they emphasize the present—the here and now—with marked success.

So begin by realizing that you are in control of your behavior. This is what counts because it is a proven fact that feelings change as behavior changes. Then you must understand that God is not even asking you to change your feelings. He never does that. Throughout Scripture He tells us the way He wants us to behave and to think. Because He created us, He knows full well that as we think rightly and behave rightly, right feelings will appear in us as a matter of course. You need to realize that God is not asking you to work up a *feeling* of forgiveness toward your mate, but He is asking you to make a choice (no matter how you feel) to forgive him or her.

Is God making selfish demands on us? Hardly! He asks us to forgive because He knows we will benefit from it. As a God who loves you and me with a fatherly heart, He desires the best for us. That *best* includes the spiritual and emotional wholeness and the physical health that spring out of a spirit of forgiveness.

Is God making an unreasonable request? Never let us forget that God forgave *first* in a way that we can neither discount nor overlook. When Jesus Christ was rejected, falsely accused, taunted, abused, tortured, then nailed to the cross to experience the most agonizing death hatred could devise, He prayed, "Father, forgive them. . . ." God asks no more, indeed, far less, of you and me. If any man ever had the right to be bitter, it was Jesus Christ. But He wasn't. He forgave instead, and established the pattern of forgiveness for all His followers from that time forth. Remember that every command of God carries a promise in its heart. Because He commands, "Forgive as Christ forgave" (Colossians 3:13), the ability to forgive accompanies the choice to do so.

Forgiveness involves three steps: (1) Using your free will to make the choice to forgive; (2) Deliberately behaving in the manner that the Lord has shown in the Bible to be right; (3) Trusting Him to do His part by renewing your mind and giving you new, transformed attitudes.

Step One: Choosing to Forgive

To help us make the choice to forgive, the Lord provides an urgent warning in the letter to the Hebrews: "Make straight paths for your feet, lest that which is lame be turned out of the way; but let it rather be healed. Follow peace with all men, and holiness, without which no man shall see the Lord: looking diligently, lest any man fail of the grace of God; *lest any root of bitterness springing up trouble you, and thereby many be defiled*" (Hebrews 12:13–15).

The one who clings to the misery of an unforgiving spirit will be crippled in the living of life, God warns. And not only will that person be troubled by the root of bitterness crowding out good things in his life, but many others will be injured by it as well.

The word *bitterness* in the Greek New Testament is *pikrias*, giving the idea of a cutting, pricking, puncturing that is at the same time pungent and penetrating. It vividly communicates the sensations of torture, and this is just what you are doing to yourself and your loved ones when you refuse to forgive your mate. Radio Bible teacher Charles Swindoll has suggested that it is like locking yourself in a concentration camp of your own making. Corrie Ten Boom describes it as sitting in a very dark room in the daytime with heavy draperies closing off the sunlight and fresh air.

You will indeed suffer by your own choice until you decide to fully and completely forgive any wrongs done to you. It may be one big thing or years of small hurts adding up to one large resentment. Certainly it will cost you something; it cost God more than we can ever know to forgive us. But once you have made the choice with your will, you will discover that you have taken a big step into freedom and emotional health and spiritual growth. You have come into what the psalmist called "a more spacious place." When you choose to forgive your husband or wife totally and wholeheartedly for any and all wrongs, you will find yourself entering the "kingdom of love." I have never known anyone who later regretted that step.

As soon as you choose to forgive with your mind and your will

198

and commit this matter to God, you free both yourself and the one who offended you from the power of the past. Then, whatever happened is historical fact, and no longer emotional fact. In a real way you have opened up the wound to the Great Physician, and you will find that His love poured on it will so heal that you will no longer feel the sting.

Recall the words the Lord Jesus used to describe His ministry. He said, "The Spirit of the Lord is upon me, because he hath anointed me to . . . set at liberty them that are bruised" (Luke 4:18). There He offers us both the deliverance and the healing. There is no bruise, no emotional wound in your marriage that the Lord cannot heal when you choose to forgive and commit this matter and your subsequent behavior to Him. No hatred can hold you prisoner when you choose freedom. No negative attitude can dominate you when you choose to let it go as an act of obedience to the Lord Jesus Christ. His love simply overpowers old resentments. It is like raising the shade and opening the window in that dark room. The sunshine floods in and dispels every corner of darkness. The air is fresh and sweet and exhilarating.

Step Two: Changing Your Behavior

We find the second step in forgiveness expressed in capsule form in Ephesians 4:31-32: "Let all bitterness, and wrath, and anger, and clamour, and evil speaking, be put away from you, with all malice: And be ye kind one to another, tenderhearted, forgiving one another, even as God for Christ's sake hath forgiven you." It is time to look into the Bible to see what mode of behavior the Lord counsels and then begin to carry it out. In this Scripture passage, God shows the process of first choosing to put away the negative attitudes, then of assuming positive attitudes and behaving in positive ways, summed up in the instruction, "Be kind. Be tenderhearted. Be forgiving."

The essence of kind treatment of your partner is to treat him or her precisely as you want to be treated. Kindness, as expressed in connection with your partner's wrongdoing, will certainly include these proofs of forgiveness. You will never use the past against him. You will never talk about it again either to him or to anyone else. You will never dwell on it in your thoughts. If you think of it in passing, you will immediately remember that it has been forgiven, just as God has forgiven you for many things far worse.

I want to emphasize this point so that there will be no misunderstanding. When authentic forgiveness takes place, your behavior will change. It must change. I am reminded of a husband whose wife was unfaithful to him a number of years ago. He says that he has forgiven her. Yet even today his behavior toward her clearly shows that he does not trust her. Obviously, this husband has never really forgiven his wife, and she is only too aware of it. You can imagine how difficult it is for love to grow in that environment.

To forgive is to say good-by forever to the pain of the past and to be rid of its effects in the present. This brings us to the third phase of forgiveness.

Step Three: Renewing Your Mind

Now is the time to forget the past and move into the future. This is possible as you allow God to do His part by renewing your mind through the Word of God, thus replacing the negatives with good attitudes that will bless your marriage relationship.

As we have already observed, this ability to leave the past behind belongs to God's people. The Christian life is all present and future. God has so designed it that the Christian can always begin where he is right now to live life in a new way—God's way. How comforting to know it is impossible for us to tangle up things so badly that God cannot work them together for our good. It is hard to understand how God can (seemingly) start over with a new set of plans dating from this moment, but He can and He will. He always responds completely in love to our efforts to follow His counsel. The biblical principle is that the steadfast love of the Lord never ceases. His mercies never come to an end. They are new every morning. Great is His faithfulness! (See Lamentations 3:22-23.)

So it is altogether possible for us to say with Paul "This one thing I do, *forgetting* those things which are behind, and *reaching forth* unto those things which are before . . ." (Philippians 3:13). Forgetting . . . reaching forth. This is the way to continue beyond that moment of forgiveness into the kingdom of love to live there for the rest of your life.

Now, you may be wondering what you can do about the negative attitudes your partner holds—the barriers he or she has erected against the free movement of love. You need to take the initiative and seek his or her forgiveness. First of all, stop doing the thing that caused the feeling of estrangement between you. Show by your speech and actions and attitudes that you are aware of your wrongdoing and would like to right it. Never use the word *if* when you are speaking to your partner about the matter. Simply admit your wrong and ask for forgiveness. This means much more than saying, *"If* I have hurt you in some way, I'm sorry." Be careful not to project any blame for the problem onto your partner. Making your mate feel guilty is one of the worst things you can do if you want to restore love to your marriage.

If after all this, your mate does not immediately respond, continue to show by your consistent loving behavior that you have forgiven on your side and that you are committed to loving your partner for the rest of your life. Remember, forgiveness can begin as a unilateral action. So let it begin with you!

Now, in spite of all we have said, you may still have some mental limitations tacked on to your scope of forgiveness. In other words, "I can forgive everything else . . . but I could never forgive my partner for being unfaithful. . . ." Or, "I could never forgive my husband for *this* or my wife for *that*. . . ." Insert any unpleasant, unthinkable situation in the blanks. You name it, I have seen it, and counseled a person with the problem—usually a Christian. Sin is sin, and every person is fully capable of committing sin. It all needs to be dealt with and forgiven whatever the category. If you are feeling bitterly disappointed in your mate, that attitude also is a signal that you need to choose to forgive. Remember that God's grace covers *every* category. The love of

201

God can cover every kind of problem. I have seen in many years of counseling that no situation is so difficult or so shocking that God cannot restore the marriage and bring glory to His name in the process.

Many people think that of all sins, adultery automatically destroys the marriage. No, it is only marriage to someone else that destroys the marriage bond. Biblically speaking, adultery need be no more destructive to your marriage than any other sin. I have seen a surprising number of Christian marriages attacked by unfaithfulness. I have also seen many of these restored in such a way that the relationship has become much better than before.

Recently a pastor said to me in reference to some very troubled marriages: "Only God could heal *those* relationships!" This is true, but God is able to heal as people are willing to apply the Word of God to their situation. When you are ready to forgive and let go of your negative attitudes, God will be more than ready to heal you and renew your love for each other. He's been waiting for that all this time!

15

How to Save Your Marriage Alone

This chapter is directed to a special group of readers: those individuals who want to save their marriage at all costs, even though they have to do it alone without any help from their partner. In fact, their partner may be actively pursuing a divorce.

If you are in this group, I do indeed consider you *special*. First, by your stand you indicate a commitment to the sacredness and permanence of marriage that is God-honoring; second, you have the courage to face your own problems instead of running from them or hiding behind false pride; and, third, you exhibit the maturity which, even when there is no response, can choose to love with a steadfast love that is tough and real, intelligent and purposeful, wholly committed to your partner's well-being.

Christian psychiatrist Paul D. Meier says that there are "only three choices for any person involved in an unhappy marriage: (1) get a divorce—the greatest cop-out and by far the most immature choice; (2) tough out the marriage without working to improve it—another immature decision but not quite as irresponsible as divorce; and (3) maturely face up to personal hangups and choose to build an intimate marriage out of the existing one—the only really mature choice to make."[1]

In your case, the moment of truth has come, for your partner probably has already ruled out the second option and chosen the first without even considering the third. The question is, What will *you* do? Surrender to the pressures of the world's way of thinking and the emotions of the moment? Or make a choice based on confidence in the eternal truths of Scripture?

The stakes are higher than one may realize at the time. One choice clearly leads to the bitterness and defeat of divorce as well as lost opportunities for blessing. "Divorce is more painful than death," a woman told me the other day, her voice husky with pent-up emotion, *"because it's never really over."* Dr. Meier says that when couples run away from their problems by divorcing and remarrying, "then there are four miserable people instead of just two. . . . Why spread misery?" he asks. "Bad marriages are contagious! Numerous psychiatric research studies have shown that when couples with neurotic marriage relationships get divorced—no matter how good their intentions may be—they nearly always remarry into the very same type of neurotic relationship they had before."[2]

When you choose the pathway of irrevocable commitment to your mate and your marriage—regardless of how troubled your relationship may seem—you will find that choice leading you into a place of *agape* love and peace and personal growth. These are just some of the rewards, for the chances are very good that you will also be able to enjoy the blessings that God has wanted to bestow on your marriage from the beginning.

I am not suggesting that the healing of a marriage is an easy process when one partner resists it. But are any easy choices open to you, after all? Torn relationships involve pain, whatever you do about them. As Peter points out in his first letter, it is far better to suffer (if suffer you must) for doing *right*, than for doing wrong. He makes it clear that God's favor and blessing shine on the one who patiently suffers, if necessary, in order to do His will. Meeting your marriage problems in a biblical manner is productive rather than pointless, and whatever hurts you encounter will be less damaging than the long-term effects of divorce would be.

"The very word *divorce* should be cut out of the vocabulary of a couple when they marry," a woman with a restored marriage said, "because God's way is so much better for anyone who is willing to give it a try."

Another woman, considering the turbulent events of the past year that had driven her to grow emotionally and spiritually while she "loved her husband back" to their marriage, said, "You know, it's been all gain for me. I'm a different person now. The process was humbling, but it was worth it!"

A man said, "During the time when I was trying to win my wife's love and hold our family together, sometimes I got so tired of rejection that I didn't feel anything except a determination to do what the Bible said and leave the results with God. The only thing I was sure of was that somehow God would work it out for my good because He promised that in His Word. I never imagined the love affair He has actually given us. He really does do more than we can ask or think!"

While these comments from the far side of the problem are encouraging, I understand that the feelings you may be experiencing right now within the problem are less than pleasant. Many others have been where you are now and can empathize with what you are going through: shock, hurt, rejection, emotional confusion, temptation to bitterness, and, of course, pressures from all sides that sometimes make you want to give up.

My heartfelt goal in this chapter is to help you clarify your thoughts, stabilize your emotions, and learn to behave in a consistent, purposeful way that will save your marriage and bring a new dimension of love into your relationship.

So, if you are willing to make a commitment to your marriage based on the eternal principles and promises of the Word of God, you can take heart and let hope grow in proportion to your commitment. Contrary to what the world believes, one person *can* save a marriage. In fact, most of the people I counsel belong in this category. Even when both come to see me, one is usually dragging the other along, in a manner of speaking, and only one really cares about the outcome in most cases.

Marriage counselor Anne Kristin Carroll says, "If you think there's no hope because you are the only one in your relationship who wants or cares enough to try to save your marriage, you are wrong!'' She adds, ''In my experience most torn marriages are brought to new life, new vitality, by the interest, basically, of only one party.''[3] This has been my experience as well. I have seen numerous marriages saved when only one partner applied biblical principles in a wholehearted commitment to the mate and the marriage.

Some have not been saved. Usually this is because the individual is convinced that nothing will change the partner—that the longstanding problem of alcoholism or financial irresponsibility or whatever cannot be solved, and he or she simply gives up. Occasionally, the partner desiring a divorce has developed such a strong emotional attachment to another person that it is not broken off *in time* to save the marriage. Often, however, this infatuation ends while the divorce is being delayed, and the unfaithful partner thanks the committed mate for standing fast and preserving the marriage. In a relatively few cases, one partner pressured by family and ''loyal'' friends, develops a deep bitterness toward the other and is actually encouraged in this hostility by parents and even, sometimes, church members so that efforts at reconciliation may be unavailing.

But in the great majority of cases, the outcome depends squarely on the committed partner's ability to behave consistently in accord with biblical principles designed by the Author of marriage. So, in a very literal sense, it is *all* up to you. You need not expect your partner to do anything constructive about the marriage if he or she wants out.

Clarifying Your Thoughts

When the Bible says, ''Gird up the loins of your mind'' (1 Peter 1:13), it means to get your mental powers in a state of alertness for proper action. You must do this without delay. Often the Lord will provide the opportunity for some quiet, uninterrupted Bible study and prayerful consideration of God's plan for your situation. You may also learn some important things about yourself during this time. When one husband moved out, his parents lovingly helped the wife by keeping the children for several weeks while she prepared mentally and spiritually for the challenges ahead.

One young wife was ready to dissolve her marriage until a friend in her garden club led her to the Lord. "I only knew two Scriptures at the beginning," the wife said, "but they were exactly what I needed: 'God is not a man, that he should lie' (Numbers 23:19) and 'With God nothing shall be impossible' (Luke 1:37).

"With those truths as a foundation I began to study the Bible, desperately trying to dig out God's purpose for marriage and all that He had to say about it. I found out for myself that if I were to obey Him, then I would have to become committed to my marriage and my husband, even though he was involved with another woman and we were on the verge of divorce.

"Coming to this decision didn't make things any easier emotionally at first, but it did show me a clear path of action, and the situation actually became less complicated because there was no more confusion about *what* to do! I refused to sign the divorce papers. I had gathered evidence identifying the other woman and proving my husband's unfaithfulness. I destroyed it all. I didn't need it anymore."

A University of Chicago professor described this generation's dilemma with the now familiar quotation: "We lack the *language* to teach what is right and wrong." But the Bible-believing Christian caught in an emotionally fraught situation does not have that problem. The language of God concerning divorce is plain enough for any reader. For example:

> For the Lord, the God of Israel, says: I hate divorce and marital separation, and him who covers his garment [his wife] with violence. Therefore keep a watch upon your spirit [that it may be controlled by My Spirit], that you deal not treacherously and faithlessly [with your marriage mate] (Malachi 2:16 AMPLIFIED).

> He replied, Have you never read that He Who made them from the beginning made them male and female. And said, For this reason a man shall leave his father and mother and shall be united

firmly (joined inseparably) to his wife, and the two shall become one flesh? So they are no longer two but one flesh. What therefore God has joined together, let not man put asunder (separate) (Matthew 19:4–6 AMPLIFIED).

As you try to gain clarity of thought concerning your marital situation viewed in light of the teaching of Scripture, I suggest that you re-read the first five chapters of this book and *search the Scriptures* that have to do with marriage. Let me remind you once more of the eternal principle that undergirds the biblical counsel we offer: *It is God's will in every marriage for the couple to love each other with an absorbing spiritual, emotional, and physical attraction that continues to grow throughout their lifetime together*. It should be crystal clear that God intends for you and your mate to picture the love-bond of Christ and His church and that you must beware of substitutes who sometimes find their way into the vacuum of a troubled relationship. Obviously, infidelity and divorce are paths that move away from God's plan and blessing. But when you pour yourself into restoring love to your marriage, you can be sure that the force of His will is at work with you in the process.

It is important to fill your mind with positive biblical input: biblical counseling, preaching, and teaching; good books and Bible-study tapes; and friends who will affirm you in your commitment to your marriage. You need to take in truth from those who are as committed to the permanence of marriage as the Bible is. And don't listen to anyone else! Develop tunnel vision in this area as Proverbs 4:25–27 commands·

> Let your eyes look directly ahead, and let your gaze be fixed straight in front of you. Watch the path of your feet, and all your ways will be established. Do not turn to the right nor to the left; turn your foot from evil (NASB).

You need to maintain this total mental commitment to the truth or you will be swamped by waves of human opinion and bad advice, sometimes from seemingly religious people.

One young man came to me, confused because he had been told

to do nothing to win back his wife. He had been told to concentrate on his vertical relationship with God. I said to him, "This is true, but you can please God only when you are doing what the Bible says you are to do. You must be right in line with God's Word. We have no other direction for this life. When we are in total accord with the Word, then we can relax and God has the freedom to work with us. He always works with us on the basis of the information that we have from His Word. So the more you know of the Word of God concerning marriage and love and His abhorrence of divorce, the more equipped you will be to let God do His full work and have His full way in your life."

"I had to take a stand on this matter of outside influence," a wife told me. "Everyone has been anxious to give me advice about my marriage. I refuse to discuss it with people who hold an unbiblical viewpoint, or people who try to turn me against my husband, or people who make me feel sorry for myself and encourage weakness in me. I can't afford to be around worldly friends anymore. They tear me down; they tear my husband down. They may mean well, but they are so misguided. I want to be with people who will stand with me and support me when I might falter."

When your mind is settled, your thoughts clarified, and your commitment made, you will find that you no longer lie at the mercy of outside events, reacting to every new circumstance with fresh pain and bewilderment. Instead, your viewpoint becomes, "This is what I am going to do, *no matter what,* because it is God's way to do it. I can count on His wisdom, and I can trust Him with the results of a course of action based on His Word."

"I'm not standing by my marriage anymore on the basis of what the outcome will be," one woman told me. "People urge me to dump my husband, give up on him because he's made my life miserable; they tell me I deserve someone better, that I wouldn't have any trouble finding someone else to love me. My answer is that marriage is sacred; marriage is permanent; I am committed by my marriage vows; I am one flesh with my husband; and then I really shock them! I tell them that even if there is no happy ending for our marriage, I will not regret the stand I have taken. I will know that I made the right decision and followed the only course possible for me. I will have done all that I could.

"But my trust is not in what I am doing," she added. "It is in God and His Word. He has a perfect, loving plan for my life, and He's wise enough and powerful enough to carry it out, if I cooperate by following His counsel. So I'm going to keep on obeying Him in my marriage and I'll leave the results with Him. I am at peace with that."

Stabilizing Your Emotions

As a medical doctor I often know when a marriage is in trouble because my patients come to me for something to alleviate their highly nervous state. One wife whose husband was intensely infatuated with someone else came to me convinced that she was on the verge of "losing her mind." She feared that she might not survive and had pleaded with her in-laws to keep her children away from contact with the other woman if something happened to her. Her mental anguish was indeed acute.

Months later I was impressed by the transformation in this woman—alert, poised, attractive, well-balanced in thought and speech, she now seemed to possess a central core of peace. Although her marital problems were not completely resolved, her husband had returned home and they were working together to build a real love relationship.

"Before he could tell me he loved me, even before he came back home, he was impressed with how I had changed," she explained. "He was in such a turmoil, and the peace and stability that I had found really attracted him to me." She opened her Bible. "Did you know that Proverbs 5:6 says an adulteress's ways are *unstable?* My husband found that out! The contrast with the spiritual maturity that I had gained the hard way inspired his respect and made him want to be with me."

"How do you account for this change in you?" I asked, although I was sure I already knew the answer.

210

"The Lord changed me through the Word of God," she said. "It was as if I were drowning, and the Word was the lifeline. I spent hours every day in the Bible. To begin with, the Lord showed me how wrong I had been as a wife. I couldn't feel betrayed and mistreated anymore; I couldn't even blame my husband for looking for someone else to make him happy when I had failed so badly. I saw that I had to change, and the Word showed me how.

"Then the Lord showed me that I couldn't be bitter toward the other woman. Bitterness was out. Love was in. And all the time the promises of the Word of God were stabilizing me, giving me a steadiness to face each new day. When something occurred that seemed like a severe setback, I could calmly go to the Word and study and begin to understand the new lesson He was teaching me.

"As *you* know," she said, "when this all started, I just had to have someone I could call day or night to talk to because I was so scared, so hurt, so desperate. But the time came when I learned to go straight to the Lord. It took a while to reach that, but it's the greatest blessing for me out of this whole experience. I've learned that all I really need is the Lord!"

This wife's testimony points the way to emotional stability for any individual who needs it—and most people faced with the disintegration of their marriage desperately need it.

In a magazine article, "Fly by the Instruments," Gloria Okes Perkins compares times of trial and emotional instability in the believer's life with the clouds, fog, and air turbulence an airplane pilot experiences. The answer in both cases is to fly entirely by the instruments.

"When there is no visual contact with the earth . . . when no horizon is in view, stability can be achieved only by depending on what those vital gyros have to say," she writes. "What is true for pilots in the skies is just as true in another sense for believers in the difficulties of life when normal conditions of stability seem to vanish in clouds of sorrow and confusion. Sooner or later every believer will have to 'fly by instruments' spiritually and emotionally through bad times. . . .

211

"While piloting a plane in a thick fog, a pilot cannot be sure of his direction unless he gives full attention to his instruments. When flying through a thunderstorm, the turbulence will throw him about, and the darkness within the clouds will threaten to disorient him. Sometimes he will feel as though he is going up or down or turning around. But he cannot depend on his feelings. Only the gyros can be trusted, so the pilot must hang on to the controls in the turbulence and discipline his mind to concentrate on the instruments while he flies through the storm.

"The parallel truth for the Christian in troubled times is clear. Undisciplined feelings . . . can cause a crash unless one keeps himself stabilized by the facts of the Word of God. . . . Every promise in the Word of God is like a gyro giving information to stabilize him in a specific situation. . . . With daily practice one learns not to panic but to believe a specific truth from the Bible fitted for his own unique circumstances. By experience one learns not to fight his feelings, but to look away from them to the 'instrument panel' of the Word of God which is utterly dependable.

"One discovers that if he will just hang on in the worst of the turbulence, no matter how disrupting, his mind and heart steadied by the great truths of the Word and his eyes intently fixed on God Himself, he will eventually break through rain-black clouds to soar once more in the clear, tranquil atmosphere."[4]

This is the way *you* can gain emotional stability at this time, no matter what your situation.

Learning to Love

We come now to the practical behavior that can save your marriage. Your challenge is to learn how to love your partner day in and day out in such a way that there will be a responding love. Remember, you become lovable by loving, not by straining to attract love. So be careful how you love. Loving your mate in God's way does not mean clinging, complaining, or making demands. Moodiness, anger, and temperamental displays will only hinder your efforts. Loving your mate in God's way does not mean playing games—trying to inspire jealousy or insecurity, playing hard to get, taking petty revenge, or any of the other approaches you may have used in your early teens that are wholly inappropriate for marriage.

I recommend that you read 1 Corinthians 13, in as many different modern English translations as you can find. Read it again and again to learn the behavior patterns that characterize the genuine loving that God can use in healing a marriage. Fill your mind and spirit with these basic behavior responses so that they can reshape your attitudes and change your actions.

One wife asked her husband, "What can I do to show you that I love you?" This was his answer: "You could be nice to me all of the time, not just when you're in the mood. You could treat me as if I were really special. You could show me that you love me by respecting me and not trying to take over."

A wife expressed her desire in this way: "I just want my husband to keep telling me that he loves me and approves of me. Not only with words but also with kisses and thoughtfulness and understanding and protectiveness. I suppose what I'm really saying is that I want him to love me the way the Bible says—to love me the way Jesus Christ loves the church!"

We all hunger to be loved. And we want tangible proof that we *are* loved. But someone in the marriage has to take the initiative and begin the loving process. When misunderstandings piled upon misunderstandings erect walls between husband and wife, this can be difficult. Robert Louis Stevenson spoke the truth when he said, "Here we are, most of us, sitting at the window of our heart, crying for someone to come in and love us. But then we cover up the window with the stained glass of pride or anger or self-pity so that no one can glimpse the lonely self inside."

Is it possible in your own marriage that two lonely people are crying out for love on the inside, yet confused about what the other really wants and feels? There is only one constructive answer. You must choose to love your partner, unilaterally at first, and show it by meeting not only his or her needs, but desires as well.

In short, you will need to apply all the principles we have

discussed in previous chapters concerning the five ways of loving and how to love. The easiest way to establish an effective habit of loving behavior is to follow the B-E-S-T prescription of chapter 13 of our book.

At one of our Christian marriage seminars in the South, a middle-aged couple came up to Gaye and me, smiling broadly and obviously happy. The wife's first words were, "We just wanted to meet the people responsible for the *Love-Life* cassette album that saved our marriage!" Taking turns, their faces radiant, they explained how they had given up on their marriage with their relationship problems seemingly insurmountable. But then a Christian counselor gave them our *Love-Life* cassette album, and they found hope for the first time. They had carefully followed our suggestions step by step and discovered that they worked. The wife reached in her purse, pulled out her billfold, and took a card out to show us. On it she had outlined the B-E-S-T prescription with a few lines under each point. She said, "I used to look at this many times in the course of a day, and I still use it daily to remind me how to love. Our marriage is so good now—I do not want to slip back into the old patterns of behavior that almost destroyed it!"

Loving your partner by blessing, edifying, sharing, and touching should become a lifetime habit. Not only does it inspire a responding love, but it will bring to life your own feelings of love and keep them alive. This occurs because feelings are determined by actions—not the other way around. If you behave as if you love someone, the *feelings* will inevitably follow in a short time. And by behaving in a positive way through the B-E-S-T plan, you can avoid the emotional numbness you would otherwise develop as a result of your mate's continued rejection.

Even while applying all the rest of the counsel in this book, if you alone are trying to save your marriage you are in a special situation that demands special measures and additional counsel. For, how can you show love when your partner is occupied with someone else? Or has moved out of the home? Or meets your love with hostility? Or totally ignores you?

The special advice I have for you will run counter to everything the worldly mind teaches, and it will go against your own nature to do it. But if you want to save your marriage, you cannot afford to indulge your pride or exalt yourself. You will not even be able to carry out this counsel on your own because only the individual with spiritual resources through a knowledge of the written Word of God and the abiding presence of the Lord Jesus Christ can consistently and effectively do what needs to be done.

The spiritual principle you must comprehend and lay hold of is this: "He (the Lord) has said to me, 'My grace is sufficient for you, for power is perfected in weakness.' Most gladly, therefore, I will rather boast about my weaknesses, that the power of Christ may dwell in me . . . for when I am weak, then I am strong" (2 Corinthians 12:9–10b NASB).

In the light of that principle, which operates in the Christian's life whenever applied, here is preparation you need to make in your purposeful effort to save your marriage.

1) Prepare for the worst, knowing you have a sufficiency of grace.

Usually when a troubled relationship exists, the mate who wants to leave either is involved with another person or anticipates involvement with someone else. So, when a person comes to me with a marriage problem, one of the first things I ask is this:

"Is your partner involved with someone else?"

Often the answer is a reluctant, "Yes, somewhat. . . ."

"All right," I say, "what would you do if your mate were involved in adultery with that person?"

"Well," the individual may say, "it hasn't gone that far yet!"

Then I explain that he or she must be prepared to face the possibility. One wife clung to the belief that her husband (an active Christian) could not possibly have gone as far as the act of adultery with the other woman (a Christian "friend"). When the truth came out, it was doubly devastating because she was totally unprepared to handle it.

Another wife began to prepare emotionally and spiritually for

215

the possibility of her husband's unfaithfulness as a result of Gaye's counsel to her at a seminar. The wife called later to tell us that her husband had come to her soon after the seminar with a confession: he had had a lengthy affair with his secretary. "I'm so glad I was prepared," the wife told us. "He wanted to stay with me, but he thought it would be hopeless once I knew the truth about his past. I had been listening to the *Love-Life* cassettes over and over again, and I was able to handle the situation with calmness and love and forgiveness. I already had my mind focused on the important thing—saving our marriage. We're going to do it."

Adultery probably is the worst sin that most mates can think of their partners committing. It is wise to be prepared practically, emotionally, and spiritually for the worst. Then other problems will become easier to handle if they are "all" you have to contend with. Prepare for the possibility of infidelity by realizing that adultery is sin—the same as any other sin, because God can forgive that individual and so can you! You must forgive if you are to be free to love and live and grow as a person.

Karen Mains, in *The Key to a Loving Heart,* vividly describes the connection between forgiveness and love:

> The key that opens the door to the locked rooms of our hearts is forgiveness. It is only when we have experienced forgiveness (. . . I mean being overwhelmed by the reality of forgiveness, being able to touch, taste, and smell its results) that we find the locks are sprung, the doors flung open, the windows tossed high, the rooms inhabited, the fires lighted on the hearths. It is then we discover that our hearts are finally free to love. They have become what the Creator intended them to be, places with immense capacity to embrace.

After you have forgiven, you must prepare yourself to cope with a continuation of the affair and decide exactly how you will handle it, even rehearsing in your mind how you will respond to certain situations that might arise. You must be prepared to respond in a loving way, even to a continuing infidelity. It's not that you are condoning it; it's not that you are ignoring it. But early on in the process of resolving your marriage problems you have to come to the powerful realization that *you* cannot reform your mate, no matter how hard you try. Your only option is to become the husband or wife God has commanded you to be in Scripture, and to apply every principle of behavior from the Word of God to the day-by-day challenges of your situation. You may well save your marriage. Without question, you will enjoy God's blessing and favor.

What will change your mate? Sometimes the change comes through a personal knowledge of the Scriptures. One Christian husband forsook his adulterous affair and came home because through personal Bible reading he realized how deeply he had fallen into sin and how terrible the results of that could be. His wife told me, "I thought he had come home because he loved me. But he admitted that he came back in obedience to God's Word. That really did something to my pride at first! My husband said, 'God promises me that He will teach me how to love you as you should be loved.' Then I realized how dumb I had been with my hurt pride. I should be thanking the Lord because this is the best way for us to begin building a real love relationship. If he had come back just because I looked more attractive to him at the moment, it wouldn't have lasted. Now, with *both* of us, our strength and hope to rebuild our marriage rests with the Lord."

But what about the mate who will not go to the Word of God for counsel? In that case, he or she must see in you a living, walking example of God's truth being applied faithfully in every situation. Never leave the impression that you are behaving this way just to change your mate. You do it because God said that you must, whether it seems to work or not.

In severely troubled marriages, it is usually the husband who comes and goes from the family home, perhaps spending part of the time with another woman. While this is obviously distasteful, I sometimes counsel wives to accept this situation on a temporary basis as it is preferable to total separation leading to dissolution of the marriage.

For this reason, your husband is given the freedom to be in both worlds for a time while he tries to live out his fantasy If you are doing your part at home, a clear contrast will become evident to him. "The lips of an adulteress drip honey, and smoother than oil is her speech; But in the end she is bitter as wormwood, sharp as a two-edged sword. Her feet go down to death. . . . She does not ponder the path of life; her ways are unstable, she does not know it" (Proverbs 5:3–6 NASB). Sooner or later, this will become apparent to your husband. You have the opportunity, if he is still coming home at least part of the time, to show him genuine sweetness with no bitter aftertaste and the gracious, stable serenity that only Christ can give. Your behavior can remind him of the continuing joy and dignity of remaining as the head of his family in contrast to the social, spiritual degradation that biblically is promised to the man who casts his lot with an adulteress. You will not accomplish this by trying, but by *being*: being the loving, gracious wife God would have you to be as defined in the Scriptures.

This is why I urge all men and women under my counseling to avoid separation no matter how serious their problems are. (The only exception is in the case of actual physical injury that could require a legal separation.) As long as the two of you live in the same household, you have the daily opportunity to put powerful biblical principles into action. Don't underestimate your advantage. You are in a position to love so unchangingly that the impact on your partner will intensify with the passing of time. As you consistently apply eternal concepts to your daily relationship, time and togetherness become your helpers in restoring love to your marriage. If you are living apart, then you must take advantage of every common bond you have, such as children or business, to display love through your behavior and attitudes.

The rule is to show him the difference when he is home; make him glad to be there! One wife described how she behaved toward her husband who was beset by financial problems and wavering between home and the other woman's apartment. "I was willing to let my husband have what we had accumulated (mostly deots)," she smiled. "But the other woman was pressuring him to leave home and telling him what she would allow him to give to his children. I thought, He's got one woman pressuring him. He doesn't need two. So I left him alone, coped without demanding money from him, and refused to charge to his accounts. Originally, in his own thinking, he had placed me in the middle of his financial problems while the other woman represented freedom to him—the fantasy of starting over unhindered. But that soon changed. He saw I was on his side—concerned about him, and trusting the Lord to provide for the children and me financially. In contrast, she was demanding expensive furniture and clothes from the best shops. Yes, it hurt to go without a new coat and see her sport a $250 model. But I had to laugh. I knew it wouldn't last long. And it didn't. He's home now—permanently. Our marriage is on a new, solid footing."

In preparing to face the worst that could assault your marriage, you must remember that people ensnared by infatuation and involved in an extramarital affair are suffering from a kind of temporary insanity. They are not thinking clearly: they may behave in totally irresponsible ways; they seem beyond the reach of normal judgment. You will have to realize that this does occur. Even this has to be accepted and dealt with in your own emotional preparation. As one wife said, "While my husband was 'out of it' I didn't try to reason with him. I didn't condemn or judge or scorn or rebuke. I just accepted him the way he was. During that period, I used the waiting time to grow in the Lord myself. Happily, my husband is back to normal now and a lot wiser than before."

When the wife in the marriage becomes infatuated with someone else she will usually move out of the home permanently or demand that her husband leave the home. I counsel the husband not to move away. There is no way he can be forced out of his home if his behavior is moderate and reasonable.

Husbands must be prepared to actively pursue their wives and win them back. But the wife should never be allowed to feel that he is doing this out of duty. Only love will have the force to prevail over the warring emotions that have brought an unfaithful wife to this point.

For instance, a church-going wife's one-time indiscretion became public knowledge. Deeply ashamed and emotionally confused, she left her husband and moved into an apartment where, in a combination of guilt, defiance, and loneliness, she continued to see the other man. Her husband had all the sympathy from their family and church friends. But was he blameless in the matter? Or had he failed to love her as he should before the act of infidelity occurred? In almost every case, the injured party has to bear some responsibility for the breakdown of the marriage. In this situation, the wife's out-of-character behavior had developed after the tragic loss of their child. The husband recognized that he perhaps had failed to exhibit the sensitive understanding he should have shown her at that time. Clearly, he had failed to meet her needs and desires.

Now he had a choice. He could let her go or he could win her back (as did Hosea in the Old Testament), restoring her to her former place of honor. I reminded him of two scriptural principles from Ephesians 5. First, he and that girl were intimately united whether they were living apart or together. As the church is Christ's body, so the wife is, in a sense, the husband's body. Public opinion and her temporary indiscretions and foolish behavior could not change that eternal fact. Second, "He who loves his own wife loves himself; for no one ever hated his own flesh, but nourishes and cherishes it" (Ephesians 5:28–29 NASB).

I counseled this husband to love his wife back to their marriage by nourishing her emotionally and cherishing her in every possible way during this upheaval in her life. "If you approach her as though you are being noble and doing her a favor, you will get nowhere," I warned. "You have to convince her that you love her, that she is valuable and precious beyond any other woman in your sight, that you need her and do not want to live without her."

Another husband had been told by Christian friends to pray and ask God to bring his wife back, then to do nothing, trusting God to work in some supernatural way.

"But your marriage relationship is to picture the relationship between Christ and the Church," I pointed out. "Jesus Christ did not stay with the Father. He came to earth out of love for us and gave everything that He had to establish the relationship with us. Look, the Bible says you are to love your wife the way Christ loves the church. That means an active, pursuing love on your part."

I say to any husband who is trying to restore his marriage that he needs to understand that the only thing that will reach his estranged wife is a convincing, consistent demonstration that he really wants *her*. He is not trying to win her back because it is the right thing to do, or because it is best for the children, or because God is directing him this way. He needs to convince her that he wants her for himself. He has realized that the qualities she has are the ones he needs the most; he feels now that he is able to become the husband he ought to be; and he is eager for every opportunity to show her that he *can* and he *will* love her.

Notice that a husband must win his wife back by initiating love and pursuing, when necessary. A wife must win her husband back by responding with love at every opportunity. This is in keeping with the biblical roles and distinctive natures of husband and wife since the Creation.

The husband who has reason to believe his wife has been unfaithful should beware of asking her for information about the affair. It is enough to accept the fact that she has been indiscreet. The more you know, the more difficult it will be to handle it emotionally.

As Dr. Carlfred Broderick has noted, "In response to an informed spouse's assertion of the right to know 'everything,' repentant mates all too often supply details so vivid and concrete that they can scarcely be set aside."[5]

At the present time I am counseling two husbands, each of whom was determined to build a new love relationship with his wife after an episode of unfaithfulness on her part. But each made the crucial mistake of discussing the affair, probing for details, and they have since been tormented by the information they obtained.

As a general rule, there should be honesty between mates, and in answer to a direct question the affair must be admitted, but details should not be revealed. Tell your partner the subject is too painful to discuss and that you are much more interested in the love affair the two of you can have in your marriage. Unless you are asked, never confess an affair from the past that would come as a shock to your partner. Confession in this case is not virtuous honesty; it is a cruel act that puts the burden and pain on your mate. Keep the knowledge to yourself, confess your wrong to God and rest in His forgiveness.

In this extensive discussion of coping with adultery in marriage, I am in no way minimizing the sin of adultery or discounting the intense suffering it causes. But Christians should be the most realistic people in the world, enabled by the resources of Christ to confront and heal the deepest problems of human relationships. Some researchers say that more than 50 percent of Americans have committed adultery at some time in their marriage. From my vantage point as a family physician for twenty-five years, this estimate sounds quite conservative! But I want to emphasize that a one-time experience of adultery or even an affair of some duration need not destroy your marriage relationship. I can second Dr. Meier's observation that while the wounds from adultery run very deep, mature human beings have a tremendous capacity to forgive one another. Dr. Meier says, "Patients have told me that they never thought they would be able to forgive their mate if he or she ever committed adultery—until it actually happened. Then they were amazed at their own ability to forgive. They realized how much they wanted to restore intimate fellowship with their mate."[6]

So, when you must face the possibility of unfaithfulness on the part of your partner, remember that the Lord has grace enough for you, not only to endure or accept the situation, but also to redeem it.

2) Prepare to be "perfect," knowing you have a sufficiency of grace.

This may come as shocking information, but if you want to save your marriage, you cannot be just a "good" husband or wife. You have to be perfect in your behavior toward your partner. You must *do* and *be* everything the Bible prescribes for your role in marriage, and you must be very sensitive to avoid anything that will set your partner off. The least slip in word or action will give your mate the excuse he or she is looking for to give up on the marriage. Since resentment and rationalization are two of the key issues in the thinking of an unfaithful partner, even one remark spoken out of turn can fan the flames of old resentments and give weight to rationalizations that the partner is manufacturing to excuse his or her behavior.

One wife said, "I had to prove over a period of time that I had changed before my husband could believe it. He kept expecting to face my anger or a miserable silence when he walked in the door. For years, I was so moody, he never knew how he would find me. But now he is beginning to realize a new pattern has formed and things are not the way they used to be."

In talking about "perfect" behavior, we must always recognize the fact that it is the Lord who makes this possible, providing the pattern, the purpose, and the power for fundamental change in our behavior and attitudes. One wife married to an alcoholic said, "I had tried for years to manipulate the situation and change my husband by my own efforts. By nature I am strong-willed and ready to fight for what I want. But I just gave up one day. I remember beginning to cry in the bathtub and praying, 'Lord, you know that I can't handle my own life. Just take over for me, because I have learned that I can't control *anything*.

"And that," she went on, "was the turning point for our marriage. For both of us! Change came slowly. But I had the opportunity to pour out my heart to my husband and tell him how much I needed to be loved and to be put first in his life. He really took me seriously. He had a new motivation to quit drinking. A friend took him to Alcoholics Anonymous, and he has not had a drink in the last seven years. He's again become the wonderful man that I married. I thank God every day for my husband's sobriety and dignity and the love and respect we have for one another now. But the Lord had to change *me* before it could happen."

Three rules should be followed as you learn to love your partner with a love that can save your marriage:

First, *consistently do everything you can to please your mate and meet his or her needs and desires*. Love your partner in such a way that it will be interpreted as love. Study what your partner needs. One wife said, "I used to work in my husband's business, and I thought I was really helping him—really impressing him with my wisdom and efficiency. After our marriage ran into deep trouble, I discovered that wasn't what he needed at all. Now I am staying at home and becoming what he needs—not a whirlwind worker, but a woman who quietly loves him and believes in his ability to handle things well."

Pleasing your partner involves action—sometimes drastic action. A striking example of this is the wife who had had endless fights with her husband over flying in their plane. He was an enthusiastic private pilot; she was terrified of flying. But when it came down to saving her marriage, she went alone to the airport and took flying lessons, trusting the Lord to remove her fears. Today she is a pilot too, and they have a better marriage than ever before. She says, "I have found that spiritual growth gives me the courage I need to change."

Second, *consistently show your mate the respect and honor commanded in Scripture whether your mate personally merits it or not*. I cannot overemphasize this. All of the scriptural admonitions concerning marriage are rooted in this one principle. Study the New Testament passages on this subject, particularly Ephesians 5, Colossians 3, and 1 Peter 3 as translated in the Amplified Bible and other modern English versions. The husband, whatever his behavior, is by position the head of the wife and is to be treated with respect at all times. The wife, whatever her behavior, as an equal heir of the grace of life, is to be given the place of highest honor and special privilege by her husband. As someone has said, she is to be treated like a Ming vase instead of an old garbage can!

Third, *totally avoid criticism of your mate*. Accept whatever your partner is or is not doing without comment or histrionics. Do not even suggest a secret disapproval. Again, the New Testament provides an abundance of instruction. In Colossians 3, for example, we read:

> Clothe yourselves therefore . . . [by putting on behavior marked by] tenderhearted pity and mercy, kind feeling, a lowly opinion of yourselves, gentle ways, [and] patience—which is tireless, long-suffering and has the power to endure whatever comes, with good temper. Be gentle and forbearing with one another and, if one has a difference (a grievance or complaint) against another, readily pardoning each other; even as the Lord has freely forgiven you, so must you also [forgive]. And above all these [put on] love and enfold yourselves with the bond of perfectness—which binds everything together completely in ideal harmony. And let the peace (soul harmony which comes) from the Christ rule (act as umpire continually) in your hearts. . . . And be thankful—appreciative, giving praise to God always (Colossians 3:12–15 AMPLIFIED).

3) Prepare to be rejected, knowing you have a sufficiency of grace.

What about rejection while you are trying to carry out these principles of love? I can only say that Jesus Christ was perfect and He was rejected! We should not be surprised when it happens to us. But do not give up your efforts because of rejection. One husband told me how he had sent a Valentine's Day flower arrangement to his estranged wife with a card from himself and their little girl. When he came home from work that night, the flowers were on the front step waiting for him—returned in scorn. Later, when she called him at his business, he told her, "I just want you to know that I love you. The hatred you are throwing at me right now cannot change that. I've discovered since we separated that my love for you has much higher limits than I ever realized."

She was quite taken aback by the loving way he had responded to her rejection of his gift. She said, "But you wouldn't want to live with a woman who doesn't love you?"

He answered, "Honey, love is something that doesn't grow overnight, especially when it has been treated the way both of us

225

have treated our relationship in the past. You can't buy love. You aren't born with it. It's something you work at and build together. We haven't even tried that yet.''

A happy wife wrote me a note of thanks for my counsel which gave her the courage to stick with her marriage. She said, ''One little thing you said to me meant so much. You said, 'So what if your husband doesn't tell you he loves you right now!' I knew you were right. It really wasn't that important.'' This wife found that putting up with a little rejection was worth it in the long run in order to have a revitalized marriage.

I have talked with many women who tell me that when they do not feel their husband's love, the Lord has a way of loving them that is almost tangible. ''Like being in the sunshine, just feeling the warmth of His love,'' several wives agreed. A lovely young wife carried that a step further in her own trying situation. She said that it was often difficult dressing to go out for the evening with her husband because she knew in advance that he would not treat her the way she longed to be treated. So she developed the habit of thinking of the Lord Jesus as her friend and escort for the evening. ''It helped me tremendously,'' she said. ''I looked my best for Him, I behaved my best for Him, and I was constantly aware of His steadying presence with me!''

In summary, you need to give love to your mate biblically, emotionally, and physically whether you receive a response or not. This is altogether possible through *agape* love. One wife, whose husband was involved with another woman, said, ''I tried to show him that my love for him did not depend on how he treated me. I still showed him physical affection. I said to him sometimes, 'I love you, no matter what you are doing right now, and I believe the Lord means for us to be together.' I sent him little cards with appropriate messages that expressed my caring while we were apart. And, do you know, when we reconciled, I found that he had saved every one of them!''

I asked some wives who had been through the experience to give me their list of do's and don'ts for any woman trying to save her marriage. Here are the excellent suggestions they compiled:

226

- There can be no growth in your relationship as long as there is doubt as to your commitment to your marriage. Make your commitment!
- When your husband withholds his love, trust the Lord to meet your emotional needs. He won't let you down!
- Give your husband honor, love, and biblical respect even though his actions do not deserve it. Give him warm acceptance no matter what. The more hopeless your situation is, the more your loving behavior is apt to be accepted as genuine.
- Don't try to reform your husband. Just love him.
- Live one day at a time.
- Don't try to do it on your own. The Lord is with you!
- Don't be bitter against anyone in the situation. Never turn your children against their father. Forgive!
- Don't ask family or friends to take sides against your husband.
- Don't discuss your intimate marriage problems. Don't give fuel to gossip. Confide in the Lord, your counselor, and perhaps a close Christian friend whom you can trust to keep silence.
- Choose your biblical counselor wisely. *Never* discuss your problems with a friend of the opposite sex.
- Spend as much time in the Word of God as possible.
- Concentrate on yourself, redeeming the mistakes you have made, and asking God to show you how to change, rather than concentrating on your partner's failures.
- Do not separate. Encourage your husband to stay in the home, no matter what.
- Do not give your husband a divorce. Do all in your power to delay or prevent it. If you must consult a lawyer, make it clear to the lawyer that it is only for your financial protection and that of your children. Find a Christian lawyer who will help you preserve your marriage.
- Spend your time with people who will encourage you in spiritual growth.
- Do not overcompensate with your children. They need your love and stability while their father is gone, but they still need

227

discipline. It will be hard to build a new love relationship with your husband when he does come home if the children are out of control.

- Do not try to defend yourself from gossip or criticism. Keep your mouth shut. The Lord will fight for you and you will hold your peace.
- Remember that the most innocent thing you say will get twisted. Avoid loose talk and do not listen to tale-bearing.
- When you do anything (large or small) to pull the marriage apart, you are going against God's will. Let that be your guideline for all decisions.
- Don't expect your husband to change overnight when he does come back home.
- The hardest time may be when you are reconciled and you have a tendency to fall back into old habit patterns. Don't do it!
- Hope all things, believe all things, endure all things.

The Book of Hosea in the Old Testament gives us the ultimate pattern for a love without limits which eventually reunites husband and wife in spite of great obstacles. This holds particular meaning for the husband whose wife has left him for someone else. Read the following narrative account of the love story of Hosea and ask God to strengthen your own resolve through this retelling of His Word.

The Love Story of Hosea

(A first person narrative expository dramatic sermon by Dr. John W. Reed, Associate Professor of Practical Theology, Dallas Theological Seminary. Used by Permission)

I have been called the prophet of the broken heart, but I would rather be remembered as the prophet of love and hope. I am Hosea, prophet of God to Israel, my homeland.

Come with me to my home on the outskirts of Samaria. There beneath the oak tree is Gomer, my wife; I love her as I love my own life. You will learn to love her too. Sitting beside her is our son, Jezreel. He is eighteen now, handsome and strong—a young man with a heart for God. At Gomer's feet and looking up at her is Ruhamah, our daughter. Do you see how her raven hair glistens? She is the image of her mother. She was sixteen just half a year ago. And then Ammi, her brother—fifteen and as warm and bubbling as the flowing brook that you hear in the background.

We are happy and at peace. It has not always been so.

I began my ministry as a prophet almost thirty years ago during the reign of Jeroboam II. Those were years of prosperity. The caravans that passed between Assyria and Egypt paid taxes into Jeroboam's treasury and sold their goods in our midst. But they also left their sons and daughters and their gods. These gods and the gods of the ancient Canaanites and of Jezebel have wooed the hearts of my people. Altars built for sin offerings have become places for sinning.

If you were to walk through my land today, you would see images and altars in all the green groves. My people have many sheep and cattle. Some think that Baal, the so-called fertility god, is the giver of lambs, of calves, and the fruit of the field. Every city has its high place where Baal is worshiped. There is a high place not far from here—you are never far from a high place in Israel in these days! Sometimes at night we hear the beat of the priest's music and the laughter of the sacred prostitutes. Last week a man and woman who live three houses from us sacrificed their infant son to Baal.

You may wonder how Jehovah's people could sink to such unholy ways. It is because the priests of God have departed from Him. They delight in the sins of the people; they lap it up and lick their lips for more. And thus it is "Like priests, like people." Because the priests are wicked, the people are too. Surely God will judge. My beautiful land is just a few short years from being crushed under the iron heel of the Assyrian military might.

Yes, thirty years ago God appointed me a prophet in Israel. My father, Beeri, and my honored mother had taught me early to fear Jehovah, the One true God of Israel. They taught me to hate the calf deity of the first Jeroboam. Daily we prayed. Daily we longed to return to the Temple in Jerusalem. Daily we sang the songs of David and hungered for the coming of Messiah.

My ministry has always been hard. The first ten years were the hot-blooded days of my twenties. My sermons were sermons of fire. My heart bled for my people. I was little heeded and generally scorned. When I was thirty-two, God stirred me and I spent many days in prayer and meditation. I felt lonely and in need of a companion.

The first frosts of fall had tinted the leaves when I went with my parents to visit the home of Diblaim. In the busy activity of my ministry I had not seen the family for several years. We were engaged in lively conversation when through the door swept a young woman, Gomer, the daughter of Diblaim. I remembered her as a pretty and somewhat spoiled child. But now she was a hauntingly beautiful woman. Her ivory face was framed in a wealth of raven black hair. I found myself fascinated by her striking beauty and had great difficulty in turning my eyes from her.

As we returned to our home that day, my father and I talked of many things. Yet, in my mind hung the image of a raven-haired Israelite. My father's friendship with Diblaim flourished and often I journeyed with him to visit. I was strangely drawn to Gomer. Diblaim and my father talked incessantly. Then one day my father astounded me with the proposal, "Hosea, it is my desire that you should marry Gomer." I did not question that I loved Gomer. But something about her troubled me. As most young women of her time she had a love for expensive clothing, jewelry and cosmetics. That I accepted as part of her womanhood. But she seemed somehow to be experienced beyond her years in the ways of the world.

Yet, I loved her. It was my father's will that I should marry her. I knew that my burning love for Jehovah would win her from any wanton ways. God confirmed to me that indeed Gomer was His choice as well.

I wooed her with the passion of a prophet. God had given me the gift of poetry and I flooded Gomer with words of love.

She responded to my love. We stood together beneath the flower-strewn canopy of the Hebrew marriage altar and pledged eternal love to God and to each other. We listened together to the reading of God's laws of marriage. We heard the reminder that our marriage was a symbol of the marriage between Jehovah and Israel, His wife.

I took Gomer to my home. We read together the Song of Songs which is Solomon's. We ate the sweet fruit of its garden of love. She was as refreshing to me as the first fig of the season. Gomer seemed content in the love of God and of Hosea. I looked forward to the future with hope.

Shortly after the anniversary of our first year of marriage Gomer presented me with a son. I sought God's face and learned that his name was to be Jezreel—a name that would constantly remind Israel that God's judgment was surely coming. It was a stark reminder to me of the times in which we lived.

With the birth of Jezreel, Gomer seemed to change.

231

She became distant and a sensual look flashed in her eye. I thought it a reaction to the responsibility of caring for our son. Those were busy days. The message of God inflamed me and I cried out throughout the land.

Gomer was soon with child again. This time a daughter was born. I learned from God that she was to be named Lo-Ruhamah. It was a strange name and troubled me deeply for it meant, "Not loved." For God said, "I will no longer show my love to the nation of Israel, that I should forgive her."

. Gomer began to drift from me after that. Often she would leave after putting the children to bed and not return until dawn. She grew worn, haggard, and rebellious. I sought every way possible to restore her to me, but to no avail. About eighteen months later a third child was born, a boy. God told me to call him, Lo-Ammi—meaning, "Not my people." God said to Israel, "You are not my people, and I am not your God." In my heart a thorn was driven. I knew that he was not my son and that his sister was not the fruit of my love. Those were days of deep despair. I could not sing the songs of David. My heart broke within me.

After Lo-Ammi was weaned, Gomer drifted beyond my reach—and did not return. I became both father and mother to the three children.

I felt a blight upon my soul. My ministry seemed paralyzed by the waywardness of my wife. My prayers seemed to sink downward. But then Jehovah stirred me. I came to know that God was going to use my experience as an illustration of His love for Israel.

Love flamed again for Gomer and I knew that I could not give her up. I sought her throughout Samaria. I found her in the ramshackle house of a lustful, dissolute Israelite who lacked the means to support her. I begged her to return. She spurned all my pleadings. Heavy-hearted, I returned to the children and mourned and prayed. My mind warmed with a plan. I went to the market, bought food and clothes for Gomer. I bought the jewelry and the cosmetics she loved so dearly. Then I sought out her lover in private. He was suspicious, thinking that I had come to do him harm. When I told him my plan, a sly smile crept over his face. If I could not take Gomer home, my love would not let me see her wanting. I would provide all her needs and she could think that they came from him. We struck hands on the bargain. He struggled home under his load of provisions. I followed in the shadows.

She met him with joy and showered him with love. She told him to wait outside the house while she replaced her dirty, worn apparel with the new. After what seemed hours, she reappeared dressed in radiant splendor, like the Gomer I saw that first day at the home of her father. Her lover approached to embrace her, but she held him off. I heard her say, "No, surely the clothes and food and cosmetics are not from your hand but from the hand of Baal who gives all such things. I am resolved to express my gratitude to Baal by serving as a priestess at the high place."

It was as if I were suddenly encased in stone. I could not move. I saw her walk away. She seemed like the rebellious heifer I had seen as a youth in my father's herd. She could not be helped but would go astray. The more I tried to restore her the further she went from me. Feeble with inner pain, I stumbled home to sleepless nights and days of confusion and grief.

Gomer gave herself with reckless abandonment to the requirements of her role of priestess of Baal. She eagerly prostituted her body to the wanton will of the worshipers of the sordid deity.

My ministry became a pilgrimage of pain. I became an object of derision. It seemed that the penalty for the sin of Gomer—and of all my people—had settled upon me.

I fell back upon Jehovah. My father and mother helped me in the care and instruction of the three children. They responded in love and obedience. They became the Balm of Gilead for my wounded heart. The years passed as I sounded the burden of God throughout the land. Daily I prayed for Gomer and as I prayed love sang in my soul.

She was my nightly dream and so real that upon waking I often felt as if she had just left me again.

The years flowed on but the priests of Baal held her in their deadly clutch.

It was just over a year ago that it happened. The blush of spring was beginning to touch our land. In the midst of my morning hour of meditation, God seemed to move me to go among the people of Samaria. I was stirred with a sense of deep anticipation. I wandered through the streets.

Soon I was standing in the slave market. It was a place I loathed. Then I saw a priest of Baal lead a woman to the slave block. My heart stood still. It was Gomer. A terrible sight she was to be sure, but it was Gomer. Stark naked she stood on the block. But no man stared in lust. She was broken, haggard; and thin as a wisp of smoke. Her ribs stood out beneath the skin. Her hair was matted and touched with streaks of gray and in her eye was the flash of madness. I wept.

Then softly the voice of God's love whispered to my heart. I paused, confused. The bidding reached thirteen shekels of silver before I fully understood God's purposes. I bid fifteen shekels of silver. There was a pause. A voice on the edge of the crowd said, "Fifteen shekels and an homer of barley."

"Fifteen shekels, an homer and half of barley," I cried. The bidding was done.

As I mounted the slave block, a murmur of disbelief surged through the crowd. They knew me and they knew Gomer. They leaned forward in anticipation. Surely I would strike her dead on the spot for her waywardness. But my heart flowed with love.

I stood in front of Gomer and cried out to the people. "God says to you, 'Unless Israel remove her adulteries from her, I will strip her as naked as the day that she was born. I will make her like a desert and leave her like a parched land to die of thirst.'"

I cried to a merchant at a nearby booth, "Bring that white robe on the end of the rack."

I paid him the price he asked. Then I tenderly drew the robe around Gomer's emaciated body and said to her, "Gomer, you are mine by the natural right of a husband. Now you are also mine because I have bought you for a price. You will no longer wander from me or play the harlot. You must be confined for a time and then I will restore you to the full joys of womanhood."

She sighed and fainting fell into my arms. I held her and spoke to my people, "Israel will remain many days without king or prince, without sacrifice or ephod. Afterward Israel will return and seek the Lord her God and David her king. She will come trembling to the Lord and to his benefits in the last days. And where it was said of Israel, 'Lo-Ru-hamah—you are not loved,' it will be said Ruhamah—you are loved.' For the love of God will not give you up, but pursue you down your days. And where Israel was called, 'Lo-Ammi, you are not my people,' it will be said, 'Ammi, you are the people of the living God,' for I will forgive you and restore you."

I returned home with my frail burden. I nursed Gomer back to health. Daily I read to her the writings of God. I taught her to sing the penitential song of

David and then together we sang the songs of David's joyful praise to God. In the midst of song I restored her to God, to our home, to our children.

Do you not see how beautiful she is? I have loved her always, even in the depth of her waywardness because my God loved her. Gomer responded to God's love and to mine. She does not call me "my master" but "my husband." And the name of Baal has never again been on her lips.

Now my people listen to my message with new responsiveness for I am a prophet that has been thrilled with a great truth. I have come to know in the depth of my being how desperately God loves sinners. How deliberately He seeks them! How devotedly He woos them to Himself!

16

Resources for Change

Lovers never seem to tire of sharing tender reminiscences about their love affair: the intrigue of first meeting . . . the sweet moment when they confessed their caring . . . the thrill of their surrender to each other.

Intimate conversations of this nature are recorded in Scripture in the Song of Solomon. For example, when Shulamith and her beloved husband are vacationing in the countryside, Shulamith says, "Do you remember where our love began? Under the legendary sweetheart tree, of course, where every love begins and grows . . . Neither did our love begin without the pain, the fruitful pain of birth. . . ."

Of course, such reminiscences lead to a quickened desire for physical expression of their love: "O, my darling lover, make me your most precious possession held securely in your arms, held close to your heart," Shulamith whispers.

But the lovers are irresistibly drawn to speak of the quality of the love they share: its strength and its ultimate source. "True love is as strong and irreversible as the onward march of death," Shulamith says. "True love never ceases to care, and it would no more give up the beloved than the grave would give up the dead. *The fires of true love can never be quenched because the source of its flame is God himself.*"

These are the fires that I pray will be set ablaze in your own marriage!

My personal message to you in these pages has been that you and your mate do not have to live together in boredom or separate in misery. The alternative: to become *lovers* through the resources of what I will call *ultimate* love. This is what I would have you to focus on in this final chapter of *Love-life*.

In marriage, the delights of all the human loves are mingled and made fragrant as a garden when ultimate love permeates the relationship. Even more important, the human loves are stabilized by the abiding presence of ultimate love. Feelings are momentary; ultimate love is lasting. The emotions of love are like those of other natural energies, always ebbing and flowing, even as the metabolic rate of the body incessantly changes, or the wind rises and falls. No passion endures on a consistent level. But your experience of love can be so reinforced by the tensiled strength of ultimate love that you will keep on loving and continue growing in love, no matter what your marriage must face in the course of a lifetime.

The Bible teaches (and in honesty we must agree) that we cannot save ourselves by any method: the Son of God had to become the Man Jesus, to live a perfect life, die for our sins, and live again in order to save us. Equally so, we cannot truly love by our own efforts. Again, God who is Love intervenes by giving us the priceless gift of ultimate love to be poured out to others.

Your own marriage partner should be the first, last, and in-between recipient of ultimate love. It is this that will save, restore, transform, and bless your marriage beyond your highest hopes.

How is this love expressed in human relationships—this love beyond which there is no other? We have described its qualities in other chapters, but let us take one more look from a different perspective. We can search out love's characteristic behavior by reading the letters the apostles wrote to believers of the early church. For example, if we read 2 Corinthians 12 we will find these qualities of love shining through the pages, and these are the very attitudes and actions that should be pervading our own marriage:

- Ultimate love pursues the beloved. It is a love of action that perseveres against great odds and never gives up. "I come to you," Paul writes.
- Ultimate love is unselfish—undemanding and compassionate. "I will not be a burden to you," Paul says.
- Ultimate love values the beloved. "I do not seek what is yours, but *you*," Paul reassures.
- Ultimate love freely assumes responsibility for the welfare of the beloved. "I am responsible for you," Paul states.
- Ultimate love gives to the limit without totaling the cost. "I will gladly spend and be expended for you," Paul affirms.
- Ultimate love grows in expression and does not diminish, regardless of the nature of the response. "I will love you the more," says Paul.
- Ultimate love is pure in motive and action, unadulterated by self-centered considerations. "I will not take advantage of you," Paul promises. "I will not exploit you. Everything I do is for your strengthening and building up."

Surely this love is fitted for the hard realities of life! When two people love this way, their marriage is touched by heaven despite the earthly problems from which no people are exempt.

Do you want to love and be loved like this? God is the only source of ultimate love; His is the power supply that feeds the fires of true love between husband and wife. It will not be enough to learn *about* God and this love. You must learn *from* Him and become linked to Him in an eternal relationship through new life in Jesus Christ.

Let me explain how this occurs. Romans 10:9–10 says, "If thou shalt confess with thy mouth the Lord Jesus, and shalt believe in thine heart that God hath raised him from the dead, thou shalt be saved. For with the heart man believeth unto righteousness; and with the mouth confession is made unto salvation."

The Bible teaches that the Lord Jesus Christ is the Son of God who came to earth through the miracle of the virgin birth. He lived a perfect life as a man and, at a specific moment in history,

He died on a cross to bear the sins of the whole world—the sins of every individual who will ever live. He died for you personally! Through that mighty act He paid the death penalty for sin and opened the way whereby your sins and mine can be forgiven and remembered no more.

After three days in the grave, Jesus demonstrated to all people for all time that He is God by rising from the dead—a legally authenticated fact of history. After more than a month spent on this earth in His resurrection body, He ascended to heaven with all power and authority in His possession. It is written in John 1:12: "But as many as received him, to them gave he power to become the sons of God, even to them that believe on his name."

Colossians 1:13–14 explains that the Father "hath delivered us from the power of darkness, and hath translated us into the kingdom of his dear Son: in whom we have redemption through his blood, even the forgiveness of sins."

Second Corinthians 5:17–18 promises that "Therefore if any man be in Christ, he is a new creature: old things are passed away; behold, all things are become new. And all things are of God, who hath reconciled us to himself by Jesus Christ. . . ."

Salvation and new life come through believing in Jesus Christ, the Son of God, as your Savior and receiving Him by faith. You must believe these things in your heart, then confess them with your mouth—both to God and to men.

Here is a prayer that you may wish to follow in expressing your faith in Jesus Christ as your Savior:

Heavenly Father, I realize I am a sinner and cannot do one thing to save myself. Right now I believe Jesus Christ died on the cross, shedding His blood as full payment for my sins—past, present, and future—and by rising from the dead He demonstrated that He is God. As best I know how, I am believing in Him, putting all my trust in Jesus Christ as my personal Savior, as my only hope for salvation and eternal life. Right now I am receiving Christ into my life, and I thank You for saving me as You promised, and I ask that You will give me increasing faith and wisdom and joy as I study and believe Your Word. For I ask this in Jesus' name. Amen.

When we put our trust in Jesus Christ and our lives link up with His, we become new people. Our problems may seem the same, but our ability to cope with them is all new. We have suspected that we needed to change. Now we can face it and draw on new resources to effect that change.

We as Christians have a source of love beyond ourselves. We have a sufficiency of grace for every situation. We have a new kind of strength—the power of the Lord Jesus Christ—that manifests itself through our own weakness. We now have the ability to behave in the ways that will bring order and blessing into our lives. It is now possible for us to apply every biblical principle concerning marriage and to resolve relationship problems with those closest to us.

As Christian psychiatrist Frank B. Minirth has observed, "Christian counseling is unique because it depends not only on man's willpower to be responsible, but also on God's enabling, indwelling power of the Holy Spirit to conquer man's problems. I do not wish to imply that man has no responsibility for his actions, for he does; and many Christians choose to act irresponsibly. However, our willingness and attempts to be responsible must be coupled with God's power. Through God's power, man need no longer be a slave to a weak will, his past environment, or social situations. Problems do not disappear when one accepts Christ, but there is a new power to deal with them."[1]

The chances are good that you have read this book through to the end because you are hungering for a change in your marriage. You have, no doubt, seen many areas of your life that cry out for improvement. And, by now, you have realized that change must occur within yourself before you can hope for your partner to change. You know for a certainty that running away from your problems will not cause change within. You can go a thousand miles away, start a new life, get a divorce, remarry, and you will still find yourself on the old emotional treadmill, facing compounded problems and an even greater need to change.

But if you have trusted Jesus Christ as your Savior, the answers are within your grasp. You do not have to run away from yourself or your problems any longer. The question now is not: *Can* I change? but *Will* I change?

No writer has made this point more clearly than Charles (Chuck) Swindoll, radio Bible teacher, in a column entitled "CAN'T OR WON'T?" He writes:

No offense, but some of you don't have any business reading this today. Normally, I do not restrict my column to any special group of people. But now I must. This time it is *for Christians only.* Everything I write from now to the end is strictly for the believer in Christ. If you're not there yet, you can toss this aside because you lack a major ingredient: the power of God. Non-Christians are simply unable to choose righteous paths consistently. That divine response upon which the Christian can (and *must*) draw is not at the unbeliever's disposal. That is, not until personal faith in Jesus Christ is expressed.

But if you know the Lord, you are the recipient of limitless ability . . . incredible strength. Just read a few familiar lines out of the Book, *slowly* for a change:

I can do all things through Him who strengthens me (Philippians 4:13).

. . . "My grace is sufficient for you, for power is perfected in weakness." Most gladly, therefore, I will rather boast about my weaknesses, that the power of Christ may dwell in me (2 Corinthians 12:9).

For this reason I bow my knees before the Father . . . that He would grant you, according to the riches of His glory, to be strengthened with power through His Spirit in the inner man (Ephesians 4:14, 16).

. . . He has granted to us His precious and magnificent promises, in order that by them you might become partakers of the divine nature . . . (2 Peter 1:4).

And one more:

> No temptation has overtaken you but such as is
> common to man; and God is faithful, who will not
> allow you to be tempted beyond what you are able,
> but with the temptation will provide the way of es-
> cape also, that you may be able to endure it (1 Co-
> rinthians 10:13).

Wait a minute now. Did you read every word—or did
you skip a line or two? If so, please go back and *slowly*
graze over those five statements written to you, a
Christian. It's really important.

Okay, what thought stands out the most? Well, if
someone asked me that question, I'd say, "special
strength or an unusual ability from God." In these
verses it's called several things: strength, power, divine
nature, ability. God has somehow placed into the
Christian's insides a special something, that extra inner
reservoir of power that is more than a match for the
stuff life throws at us. When in operation, phenomenal
accomplishments are achieved, sometimes even *mi-
raculous.*

Let's get specific.

It boils down to the choice of two common words in
our vocabulary. Little words, but, oh, so different!
"Can't" and "won't."

We prefer to use "can't."

"I just *can't* get along with my wife."
"My husband and I *can't* communicate."
"I *can't* discipline the kids like I should."
"I just *can't* give up the affair I'm having."
"I *can't* stop overeating."
"I *can't* find the time to pray."
"I *can't* quit gossiping."

No, any Christian who really takes those five passages
we just looked at (there are dozens more) will have to
confess the word really should be "won't." Why? Because we have been given the power, the ability to
overcome. Literally! And therein lies hope in hoisting
anchors that would otherwise hold us in the muck and
mire of blame and self-pity.

One of the best books you can read this year on over-
coming depression is a splendid work by two physi-
cians, Minirth and Meier, appropriately entitled *Happiness Is a Choice.* These men agree:

> As psychiatrists we cringe whenever (Christian) pa-
> tients use the word *can't*. . . . Any good psychiatrist
> knows that "I can't" and "I've tried" are merely
> lame excuses. We insist that our patients be honest
> with themselves and use language that expresses the
> reality of the situation. So we have our patients
> change their *can'ts* to *won'ts*. . . . If an individual
> changes all his *can'ts* to *won'ts*, he stops avoiding
> the truth, quits deceiving himself, and starts living in
> reality. . . .

What a difference one word makes!

> "I just *won't* get along with my wife."
> "My husband and I *won't* communicate."
> "I *won't* discipline the kids like I should."
> "I just *won't* give up the affair I'm having."
> "I *won't* stop overeating."
> "I *won't* find the time to pray."
> "I *won't* quit gossiping."

Non-Christians have every right and reason to use
"can't," because they really can't! They are victims,
trapped and bound like slaves in a fierce and endless
struggle. Without Christ and His power, they lack what

it takes to change permanently. They don't because they can't!

But people like us? Hey, let's face it, we don't because we won't . . . we disobey because we want to, not because we have to . . . because we choose to, not because we're forced to. The sooner we are willing to own up realistically to our responsibility and stop playing the blame game at pity parties for ourselves, the more we'll learn and change and the less we'll burn and blame.

Wish I could find a less offensive way to communicate all this, but I just can't.

Oops!

Chuck Swindoll
(used by permission)

Poet and hymn-writer Annie Johnson Flint expressed the same truth in words that countless Christians have sung with grateful hearts:

> His love has no limits; His grace has no measure;
> His power has no boundary known unto men.
> For out of His infinite riches in Jesus,
> He giveth, and giveth, and giveth again!

And so some crucial choices lie before us. We must choose first of all whether to become Christians and to be linked eternally with the God of love and the Lord of life. Then we must choose whether to use the great resources He makes available to every believer.

We also determine by action or inaction the quality of love-life we will have in our marriage. It is vain to hope that a troubled relationship will get better on its own, or that somehow time will bring about more love, or that we will (accidentally?) draw closer to each other. It is up to each of us to build our house of love.

The Bible makes the choice clear in the Book of Proverbs. We are told, "The wise woman builds her house, but the foolish tears it down with her own hands" (Proverbs 14:1 NASB). "He that troubleth his own house shall inherit the wind . . ." (Proverbs 11:29) and will live to regret it.

But this need not be so! For, "By wisdom a house is built, and by understanding it is established; and by knowledge the rooms are filled with all precious and pleasant riches" (Proverbs 24:34 NASB). Our wisdom comes from a daily study of the Word of God, applying its counsel to the details of life and letting it shape our attitudes and behavior in every situation.

As you continue gathering biblical information on your role as husband or wife and learning how to love, and as learning is followed by doing, and principle by practice, you will find your obedience transformed into the passionate and joyous pleasure of loving your mate.

Isobel Kuhn in *Stones of Fire* quotes a phrase from Dr. G. Campbell Morgan that perfectly describes the uniqueness of the love-life that is available to every Christian couple:

> Principle shot through with passion,
> Passion held by principle.

This is the pattern we aim for. And as we aim we find 2 Chronicles 25:9 wonderfully true: Whatever plateau you have reached in your love-life, *"The LORD is able to give thee much more than this!"*

Footnotes

Chapter 4

[1] Silvano and James Arieti, *Love Can Be Found* (New York: Harcourt Brace Jovanovich, 1977), Preface, IX.

Chapter 6

[1] Helen Singer Kaplan, *Disorders of Sexual Desire* (New York: Simon and Schuster, 1979), p. 6.

Chapter 7

[1] Jay E. Adams, *Christian Living in the Home* (Phillipsburg, New Jersey: Presbyterian and Reformed, 1972), p. 100.

[2] Shirley Rice, *Physical Unity in Marriage* (Norfolk, Virginia: The Tabernacle Church of Norfolk, 1973), pp. 3-4.

[3] Sheldon Vanauken, *A Severe Mercy* (New York: Harper & Row, 1977, Bantam Books), p. 20.

[4] Helen B. Andelin, *The Fascinating Girl* (Santa Barbara: Pacific Press Santa Barbara, 1969), pp. 15-16.

[5] Glenn Wilson and David Nias, *The Mystery of Love* (New York: Quadrangle/The New York Times Book Co., Inc., 1976), p. 48.

[6] Mary Ellen Curtin, ed., *Symposium on Love* (New York: Behavioral Publications, 1973), p. 120.

[7] Vanauken, *A Severe Mercy*, p. 36.

[8] Mary McDermott Shideler, *The Theology of Romantic Love: A Study in the Writings of Charles Williams* (Grand Rapids: Eerdmans, 1962), p. 1.

Chapter 9

[1] Anne Morrow Lindbergh, *Bring Me a Unicorn* (New York: Harcourt Brace Jovanovich, Inc., 1971), Introduction, p. XXV.

[2] Ibid., pp. 239, 245.

[3] Ibid., pp. 248-249.

Chapter 11

[1]Kaplan, *Disorders of Sexual Desire*, p. 183.
[2]William S. Appleton, "Why Marriages Become Dull," *Medical Aspects of Human Sexuality* (March 1980): 73, 81.
[3]Jan Ensley Troutt, *Sensitivity Plus* (Rogers, Arkansas: Waggoner-Shumate Printing Co., 1979).
[4]John Powell, *The Secret of Staying in Love* (Niles, Illinois: Argus Communications, 1974), p. 188.
[5]Mary Ann Bartusis, "Falling in Love with a Best Friend's Spouse," *Medical Aspects of Human Sexuality* (February 1980): 32-43.

Chapter 12

[1]*The Anchor Bible, Song of Songs*, Introduction by Marvin H. Pope (Garden City, New York: Doubleday, 1977), p. 17.

Chapter 13

[1]Vanauken, *A Severe Mercy*, pp. 27-28.

Chapter 15

[1]Paul D. Meier, *You Can Avoid Divorce* (Grand Rapids: Baker Book House, 1978), p. 4.
[2]Ibid., pp. 5-6.
[3]Anne Kristin Carroll, *From the Brink of Divorce* (Garden City, New York: A Doubleday-Galilee Original, 1978), p. 19.
[4]Gloria Okes Perkins, "Fly by the Instruments," *Good News Broadcaster* (October 1978): 26-27.
[5]Carlfred B. Broderick, "Guidelines for Preserving Fidelity," *Medical Aspects of Human Sexuality* (May 1980): 21.
[6]Meier, *You Can Avoid Divorce*, p. 8.

Chapter 16

[1]Frank B. Minirth, *Christian Psychiatry* (Old Tappan, New Jersey: Revell, 1977), pp. 31-32.